holiday paper crafts
from Japan

holiday paper crafts

from Japan

**17 Easy Projects to Brighten Your Holiday Season
—Inspired by Traditional Japanese Washi Paper**

ROBERTTA A. UHL

TUTTLE PUBLISHING
Tokyo • Rutland, Vermont • Singapore

Published by Tuttle Publishing, an imprint of Periplus Editions (HK) Ltd., with editorial offices at 364 Innovation Drive, North Clarendon, Vermont 05759 U.S.A.

Library of Congress Cataloging-in-Publication Data
Uhl, Robertta A. (Robertta Alexandra).
Holiday paper crafts from Japan / Robertta Uhl.
p. cm.
ISBN-10: 0-8048-3691-4 (pbk. : alk. paper)
ISBN-13: 978-0-8048-3691-3
1. Paper work. 2. Japanese paper. 3. Christmas decorations. I. Title.
TT870.U47 2006
745.54—dc22

2006003724

Photography by Toshiko Kawana
Styling by Christina Ong and Magdalene Ong

Distributed by

North America, Latin America and Europe
Tuttle Publishing
364 Innovation Drive
North Clarendon, VT 05759-9436 U.S.A.
Tel: 1 (802) 773 8930
Fax: 1 (802) 773 6993
info@tuttlepublishing.com
www.tuttlepublishing.com

Asia Pacific
Berkeley Books Pte. Ltd.
130 Joo Seng Road #06-01
Singapore 368357
Tel: (65) 6280-1330
Fax: (65) 6280-6290
inquiries@periplus.com.sg
www.periplus.com

Japan
Tuttle Publishing
Yaekari Building, 3rd floor
5-4-12 Osaki
Shinagawa-ku
Tokyo 141 0032
Tel: (81) 3 5437 0171
Fax: (81) 3 5437 0755
tuttle-sales@gol.com

First edition
11 10 09 08 07   10 9 8 7 6 5 4 3 2 1

Printed in Singapore

Contents

Introduction

The Chinese invented paper dating back to ancient times. Handmade paper from Japan is traditionally dated as beginning in the eighth century. Since that early date Japan's Washi paper has become the material of the craftsman, the painter, and the calligrapher.

My Washi craft journey that began more than twenty years ago has reached another exciting high point, allowing me to share and connect with you through my second Washi book, *Holiday Paper Crafts from Japan*. The amazing part of this incredible craft adventure is that it remains uniquely new, fresh, and exciting. The Western world has just begun to touch the edges of the Washi craft explosion. Fresh experiences will only increase as the craft spreads across America and the rest of the English-speaking world. As Washi paper becomes readily available and people are introduced to the craft, it has the potential to weave its way into everyone's heart through schools, craft classes, craft stores carrying the products, and internet websites for ordering, just to name the most obvious opportunities. Elegant, beautiful, and functional, Washi paper crafts can add a distinctive touch to any event, occasion, season, or holiday need. I continue to marvel that many of the craft materials in my books are common recyclable household items (paper towel or toilet paper tube, cardboard, milk carton—the list goes on and on). Add the Washi paper and one may create an extremely beautiful objet d'art using simple throwaway items.

Through a diverse array of crafters from the Western world as well as Japan, Washi crafts on Okinawa and mainland Japan continue to provide a wonderful bridge of friendship and understanding between our cultures. The uniqueness of Washi paper is that it is handmade. The long plant fibers are intertwined during the papermaking process, producing sheets of tough and durable paper rich in warm colors and soft texture. The fibrous paper can be rolled, molded, and shaped to fit any surface, beautifying any object. There is no other paper like Washi. Japan produces many wonderful crafts using Washi paper that are seen throughout Japan and elsewhere in Asia. Students from elementary school through high school take classes in Washi crafts. Adults of all ages enjoy Washi classes also. Japan offers many elegant and beautiful Washi kit items that follow specific symmetrical and geometrical forms. It is not uncommon to see students working on Washi projects at craft stores in Tokyo and throughout Japan.

The uniqueness of my Washi experience continues to take me into the world of the abstract, helping me to develop new and exciting projects that bring Washi craft to higher levels of creativity without borders or boundaries. In this book I share some new creations and styles that hopefully will inspire others to expand and create beyond what has already been done. Washi crafts enable our cultures to sit side by side, sharing in rich and wonderful craft experiences. This is a wonderful way to communicate understanding between cultures while imparting beautiful facets of one's own culture. Even after more than two decades of working with Washi, I remain in awe of the rich heritage of Japanese Washi as it has progressed quietly and unobtrusively through the centuries of Japanese experience. It has played a key role throughout the development of the country, touching many facets of Japanese life. Withstanding the test of time, Washi presently is made only in Japan by farmers who are contracted to produce set limits of unique product. Each year the factories order fixed amounts of Washi based on orders, demands, and projected needs. The factories sell to retailers all over Japan. The network of distribution is rooted in traditions that are just beginning to reach beyond Japan and Asia.

This second Washi book is a simple how-to guide offering easy-to-follow instructions for many holiday Washi crafts. With this starting point, you will be able to create your own exceptional and beautiful Washi works of art. Brighten up the holidays with your creations of Washi paper crafts from Japan.

—Robertta A. Uhl

Shopping for Washi

All around the world, the changing seasons are marked with joyful celebration. Christmas commemorates one of the most important festivals of the year, even in Japan. Many Japanese department stores are decorated with Christmas trees, twinkling lights, and holiday music just like the stores in many other parts of the world. Even though Christians are a minority in Japan, the Japanese love festivals and Christmas coincides with many of the end-of-year events of gift giving around December and January each year.

Like all of us, the Japanese enjoy giving unique and creative gifts. The wonderful holiday gifts in this craft book will help the creative crafter to surprise friends and loved ones with handmade gifts in their favorite holiday colors.

Since Washi is the main material in all of the crafts in this book, choosing the design and pattern is particularly important. Study the craft that you would like to make and find the design and pattern that will show off the color and design of that Washi. If a pattern is too large it will disappear when making a small ornament, whereas if it is small and you can clearly see the details, it will show off the craft you are making. Likewise, if you are making a large craft, you will need to pick the appropriate paper to best highlight the larger scale of the project.

The choices are endless and often the search for the right paper is just the beginning of enjoying the creative process. You will find that there are very few traditional Christmas-themed Washi, but many of the wonderful designs and colors will work well for the holidays.

Sizes: The standard size of a full sheet of printed Washi is 26" x 39" (66 x 99 cm). Some companies make smaller sheets, so it is wise to measure the sheets before buying. Some stores sell their printed Washi rolled up in plastic packaging with the size marked on the plastic cover. In Japan, the larger craft stores display their Washi flat in drawers or loosely folded and placed on specially designed wooden shelves.

One-way patterns: Some printed Washi papers have definite one-way patterns. You will need to take this into account when doing certain projects. It is wise to buy a little extra printed Washi to ensure that the pattern is able to go in the same direction all around your project.

Economizing: When purchasing printed Washi, it is more economical to purchase full sheets than smaller pieces. If you want to have a variety of printed patterns at your disposal, try getting together with a group of friends to purchase a large number of full sheets of printed Washi that

can then be divided up among the group, sharing the expense.

Borders: Full sheets of printed Washi have a solid, unprinted border around the outer edges. These edges should not be discarded but kept for covering the holes when making Washi-covered eggs.

Internet sites: Washi has become very popular in recent years and there are a large number of Washi sites on the internet that sell Washi paper of all kinds, as well as instruction kits and books. Some of the more popular sites are www.washiart.com, www.kura.com, www.shizu.com, www.aitoh.com, www.kimscrane.com, and www.ichiyoart.com. The forthcoming site www.washiways.com will carry my books *Japanese Washi Paper Crafts* and *Holiday Paper Crafts from Japan,* selected Washi paper packets for specific craft items, kits, and supplies.

Ball Angel Ornament

A ngels—a universal symbol of peace, hope, love, protection, and goodness—will add warmth and joy to any event or holiday. This is one of my favorite crafts that I teach, and it's easy to create a vast assortment of different angel ornaments. They can be made into hanging ornaments, added to a holiday wreath, placed on top of a holiday package, or used as a baby shower gift. Invent your own angels for any special time of the year.

EQUIPMENT AND MATERIALS FOR ONE BALL ANGEL

- 4$\frac{1}{2}$" x 3$\frac{1}{2}$" (11.5 x 9 cm) rectangle of printed Washi for the wings
- 6$\frac{1}{2}$" x 3$\frac{1}{2}$" (16.5 x 9 cm) rectangle of printed Washi for the body
- 2" (5 cm) Styrofoam ball (Washi adheres better to extruded Styrofoam)
- 10mm painted wooden head bead with $\frac{1}{4}$" (6 mm) hole (or paint a face on a plain wooden bead)
- 4" (10 cm) gold or silver tinsel chenille stem for halo
- Tiny bow or rosebud
- 8" (20 cm) thick gold or silver thread or thin gold or silver cording for hanging
- Glue stick
- Small sharp scissors
- Paper clips
- Tracing paper and pencil
- Hot-glue gun and glue sticks
- 12" x $\frac{1}{4}$" (30.5 cm x 6 mm) wooden dowel
- Awl

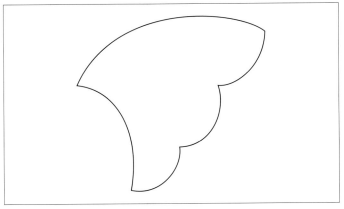

1 Trace and cut out the angel wing pattern above.

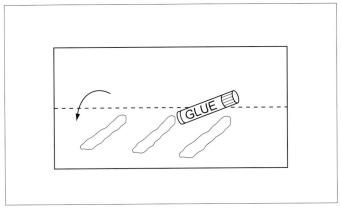

2 Fold the 4$\frac{1}{2}$" x 3$\frac{1}{2}$" (11.5 x 9 cm) rectangle of printed Washi in half lengthwise. Open it up, apply glue stick to one side, then fold back together.

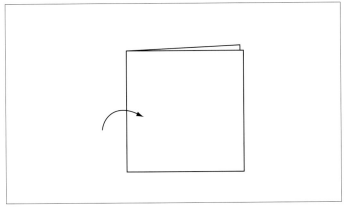

3 Fold the folded piece of Washi in half widthwise.

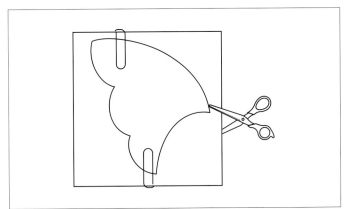

4 Place angel wing pattern on the folded Washi, secure with paper clips, and cut out. Place the cut-out wings on the table and flatten them out to dry.

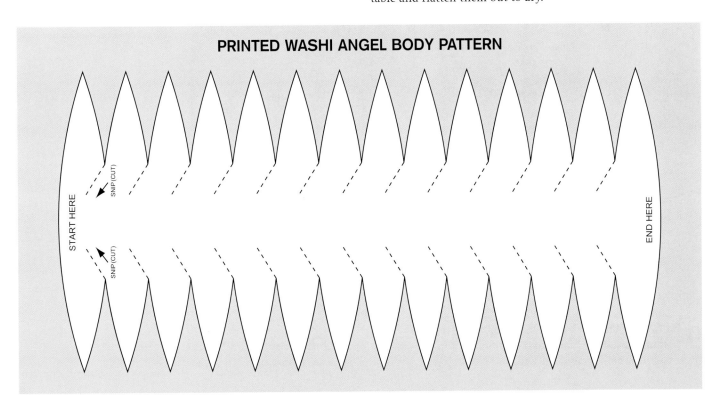

PRINTED WASHI ANGEL BODY PATTERN

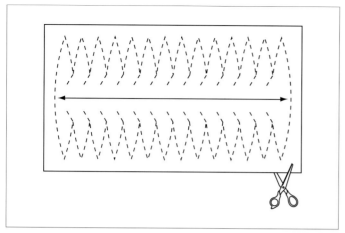

5 Trace the angel body pattern and cut it out. Paper clip the pattern to the 6½" x 3½" (16.5 x 9 cm) piece of printed Washi and cut it out.

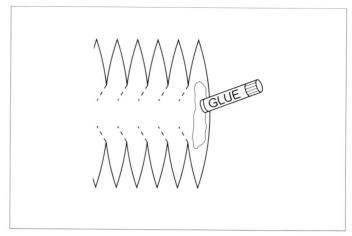

6 Apply glue stick to the first segment of Washi, starting at the end indicated on the pattern.

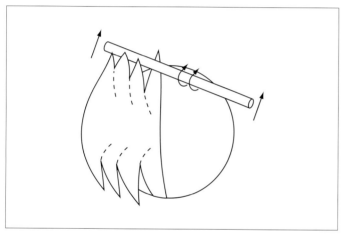

7 Center the strip on the Styrofoam ball, making sure that the ends of the Washi reach the top (north) and the bottom (south). Roll out any lumps and creases with the wooden dowel.

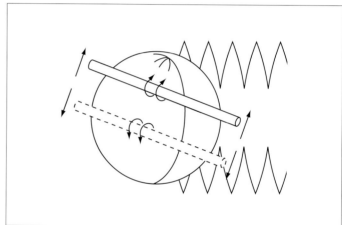

8 Continue adding segments, one at a time, around the Styrofoam ball, making sure each piece reaches the top and bottom.

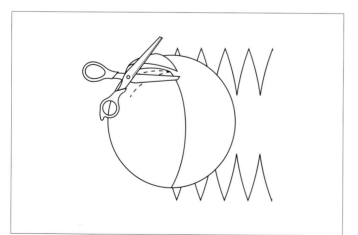

9 Halfway around the ball, start trimming the top and bottom ends of the Washi so the points meet nicely and are centered at both ends of the ball.

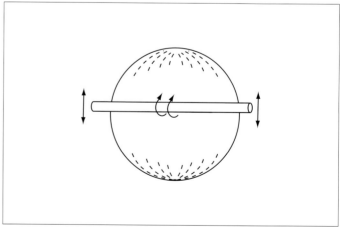

10 Use the dowel to smooth the Washi. Do not apply too much pressure when using the dowel because it may cause indentations on the soft surface of the ball.

11 Bend 4" (10 cm) tinsel chenille stem to form a small halo at one end and push the other end through the wooden bead head. Heat up the hot-glue gun.

12 With the awl, poke a hole into either the north or the south spot on the Styrofoam ball, dot with hot glue, and push the chenille stem into the hole, securing the head to the body.

13 Hot glue the angel wings at each side of the body, starting right under the head. Let the hot glue dry for a few minutes.

14 Finish off the angel ornament by hot gluing a tiny bow or tiny rosebud under the angel's neck at the front. Tie gold or silver thread or cording around the tinsel halo for hanging.

Kimono and Happy-Coat Ornaments or Magnets

One can never have enough holiday ornaments or refrigerator magnets. Washi milk carton Kimono and Happy-Coat ornaments and magnets make a colorful gift-wrap decoration. One milk carton can yield eight ornaments or magnets. This is a great craft to have ready for the unexpected gift any time of the year.

EQUIPMENT AND MATERIALS

Woman's Kimono
- 1 rectangle of printed Washi (8" x 4½" / 20 x 11 cm) for Kimono
- 2 strips of contrasting Washi (7" x ⅝" / 18 x 1.5 cm) for Kimono trim
- 2 rectangles of Washi (5½" x 1½" / 14 x 4 cm) for Obi bows (to match the Kimono trim)
- 10" (25 cm) ribbon or cording to tie Obi

Man's Happy-Coat
- 1 rectangle of printed Washi (8" x 4" / 20 x 10 cm) for Happy-Coat
- 2 strips of contrasting Washi (8½" x ⅝" / 21.5 x 1.5 cm) for Happy-Coat trim and belt

For Both
- 1 large (½ gallon / 2 liters) milk carton, washed and dried
- Small sharp scissors
- Glue stick
- Tracing paper, ruler, and pencil
- Small stapler
- Hot-glue gun and glue sticks
- 8" (20 cm) gold or silver elastic string for hanging the ornament
- 2 magnet squares or circles for each refrigerator magnet

1 Cut down all four sides of the milk carton with the scissors.

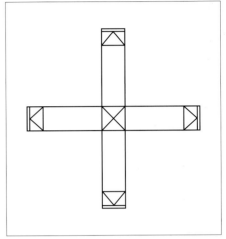

2 Open up the milk carton and lay it flat on the table, wrong side up.

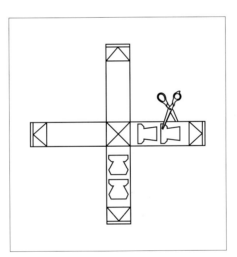

3 Copy the Kimono or Happy-Coat milk carton pattern using tracing paper, a ruler, and a pencil. Use the pattern to cut out the desired number of milk carton pieces.

4 From contrasting Washi, cut 1 strip (7" x ⅝" / 18 x 1.5 cm) for the Kimono trim and 2 rectangles (5½" x 1½" / 14 x 4 cm) for the Obi bows.

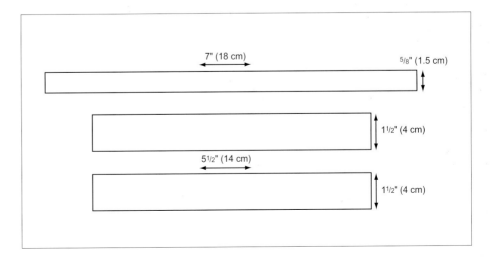

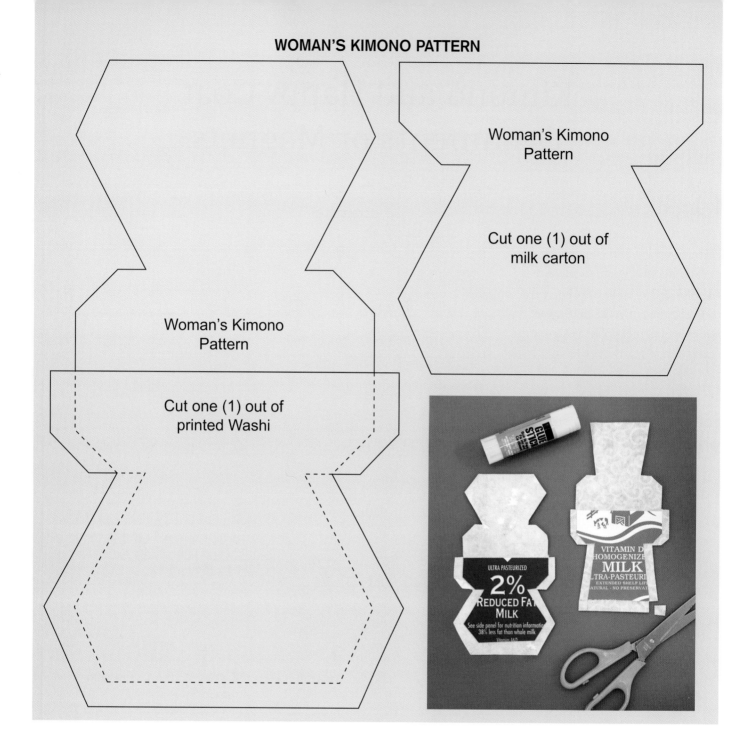

Woman's Kimono
Pattern

Cut one (1) out of
milk carton

Woman's Kimono
Pattern

Cut one (1) out of
printed Washi

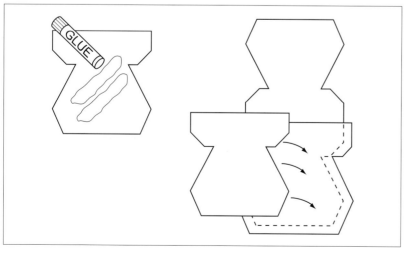

5 Apply glue stick all over the inside surface of the milk carton (the side without writing on it). Place cut-out printed Washi on the table with the wrong side facing up. Place the pasted side of the milk carton on the Washi side that is larger, making sure that it is centered. Turn over and smooth out the Washi. See photo for additional guidance.

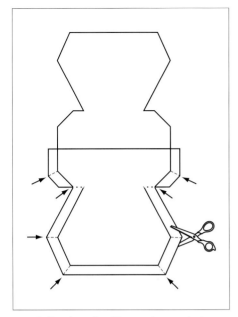

6 Following the illustration, snip (cut in) on all the sections that extend beyond the milk carton.

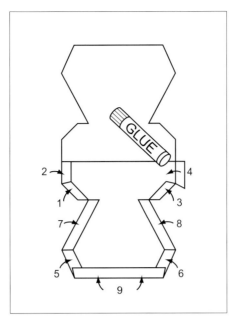

7 Apply glue stick to all extending sections. Fold sections over milk carton edges and smooth down, in the order shown in the illustration.

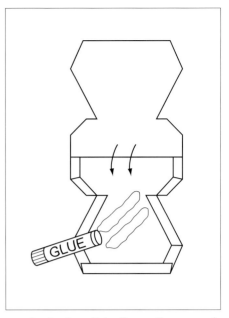

8 Apply glue stick all over the exposed side of the milk carton and the edges of Washi. Fold over the upper Kimono portion of the Washi, making sure it is even all around. Smooth it out, and if any pieces of Washi extend past the milk carton edge, just snip them off.

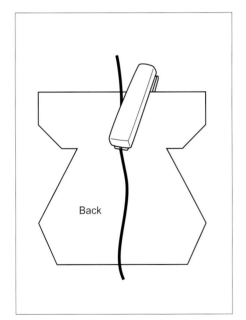

9 For the ornament only, center the ribbon, in the back, right under the sleeves. Staple the ribbon onto the Kimono.

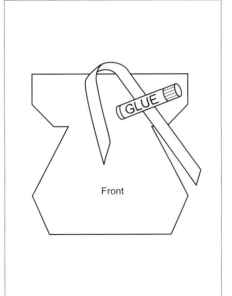

10 Fold the long thin strip of Washi lengthwise and glue closed. Turn Kimono over to the front side and glue down the long strip (first snip the tip off at an angle). Start at the center front, covering the staple, then go up around the neck, forming a collar.

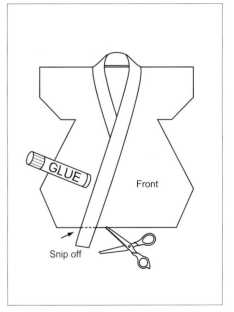

11 Continue down at an angle. At the bottom, snip off any excess trim. Follow the illustration.

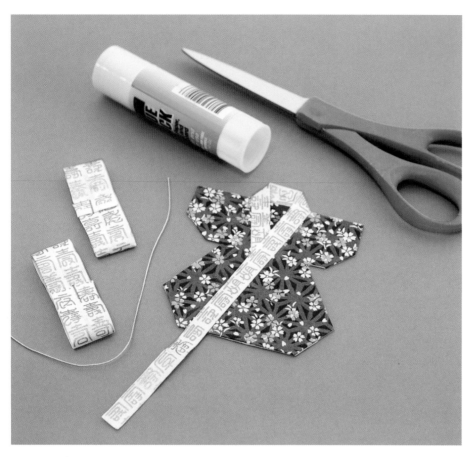

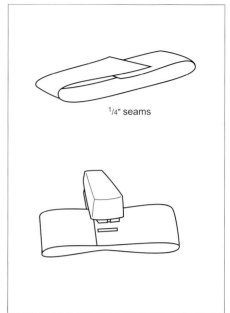

12 Fold over ¹/₄" (6 mm) seams along each long edge of the remaining two small rectangles of contrasting Washi and glue these seams down on each side. Fold the strips as shown and staple together in the middle. These will act as bows on the back of the Kimono.

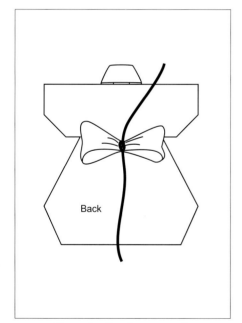

13 Place the first bow over the ribbon on the back of the Kimono, centered between the sleeve ends. Tie a knot with the ribbon to secure the bow.

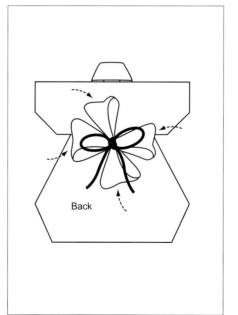

14 Heat up the glue gun. Place the second bow at an angle and tie securely with the ribbon, then tie a bow. Use the hot glue under each bow to secure them to the Kimono.

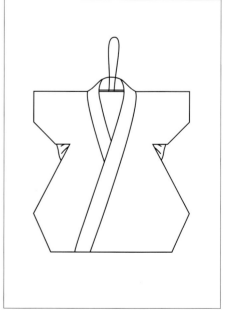

15 Tie the ends of the gold or silver elastic string together. Insert the loop into the front neck space, pass it through the knotted end, and gently pull to secure. To make a magnet, omit steps 9 and 12–14. Hot glue two magnets to the back of the Kimono.

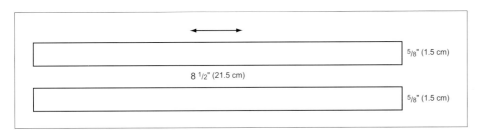

16 Cut 2 strips of contrasting Washi (8¹⁄₂" x ⁵⁄₈" / 21.5 x 1.5 cm) for the Happy-Coat's belt and contrasting trim.

8 ¹⁄₂" (21.5 cm)

⁵⁄₈" (1.5 cm)

⁵⁄₈" (1.5 cm)

MAN'S HAPPY-COAT PATTERN

Man's Happy-Coat Pattern

Cut one (1) out of milk carton

Man's Happy-Coat Pattern

Cut one (1) out of printed Washi

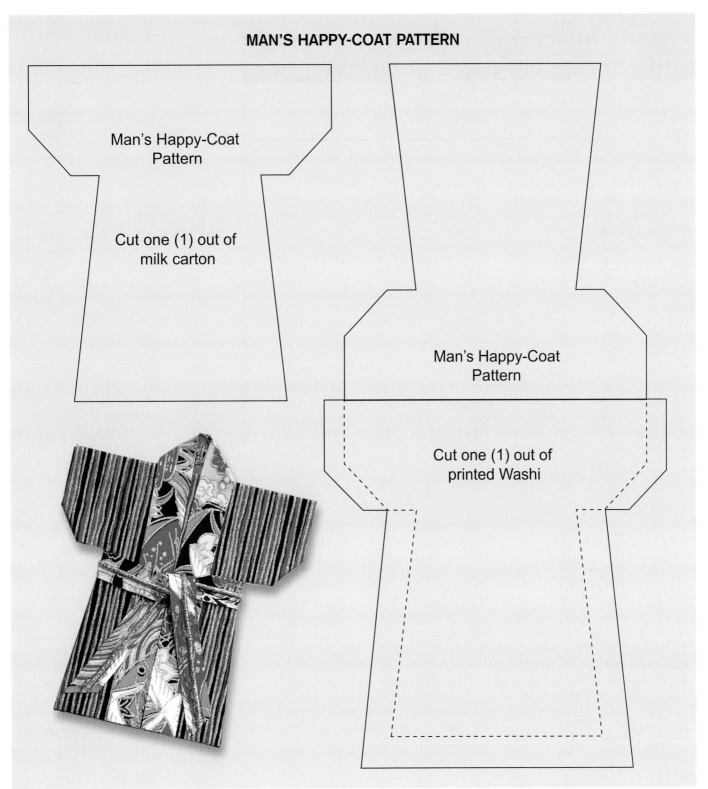

19

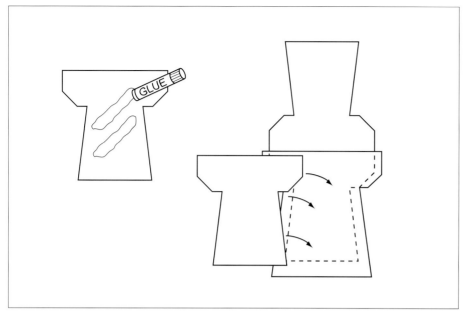 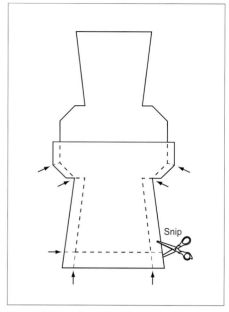

17 Apply glue stick all over the inside surface of the milk carton (the side without writing on it). Place cut-out printed Washi on the table with the wrong side facing up. Place the pasted side of the milk carton on the Washi side that is larger, making sure that it is centered. Turn over and smooth out the Washi. See photo on page 16 for additional guidance.

18 Following the illustration, snip (cut in) on all the sections that extend beyond the milk carton.

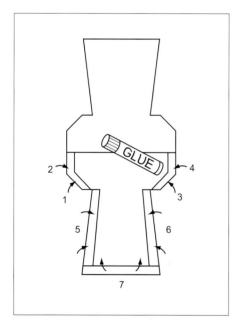 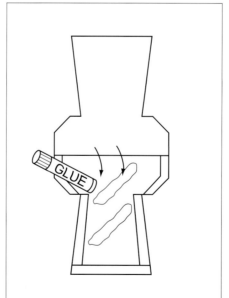 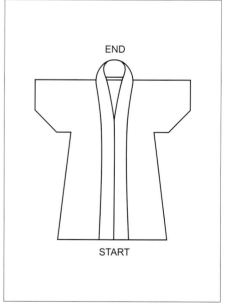

19 Apply glue stick to all extending sections. Fold sections over milk carton edges and smooth down, in the order shown in the illustration.

20 Apply glue stick all over the exposed side of the milk carton and the edges of Washi. Fold over the upper Happy-Coat portion of the Washi, making sure it is even all around. Smooth it out, and if any pieces of Washi extend past the milk carton edge, just snip them off.

21 Fold one of the long narrow contrasting printed Washi strips in half lengthwise. Use glue stick to glue closed. Following the illustration, fold the strip in half, making sure the bottom ends meet evenly. Shape the middle like a collar.

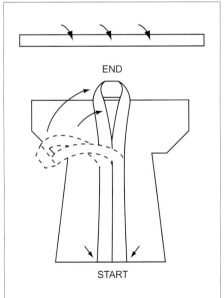

22 Starting from the center-front hemline, glue down the long strip, going up toward the neck. At the neck, separate the two strips to form a collar.

23 Fold the second strip lengthwise and use glue stick to glue closed. Place the belt around the waist, with the loose ends toward the front. Loop the ties over each other once, then glue both ends to the front.

24 Tie the ends of the gold or silver elastic string together. Insert the loop into the front neck space, pass it through the knotted end, and gently pull to secure. To make a magnet, omit the elastic string and hot glue two magnets to the back of the Happy-Coat.

Crane Ornament

The Washi crane ornament is adapted from the origami art of folding paper. The crane symbolizes long life, good fortune, and prosperity. In Japan, the crane has gained a special significance today as a symbol of peace. Washi cranes can be displayed during any holiday or special occasion, or can highlight any celebration. They are especially loved by children of all ages.

EQUIPMENT AND MATERIALS FOR ONE CRANE

- 1 square of printed Washi (6" x 6" / 15 x 15 cm)
- Gold or silver ribbon (12" x ¹/₂" / 30.5 x 1 cm)
- 1 gold or silver bell (¹/₂" / 1 cm)
- Gold or silver thick metallic string (12" / 30.5 cm)
- Thin wire (8" / 20 cm) to thread through crane
- Round pencil
- Small sharp scissors
- Hot-glue gun and glue sticks
- Awl with thin point

TIP

- Always hold and fold the Washi in the position shown in the diagrams.

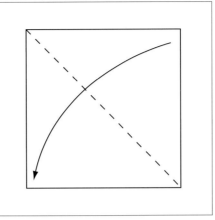

1 Place the 6" x 6" (15 x 15 cm) square of printed Washi wrong (plain) side up.

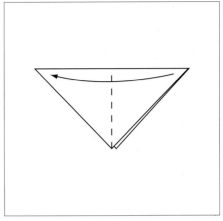

2 Fold in half diagonally.

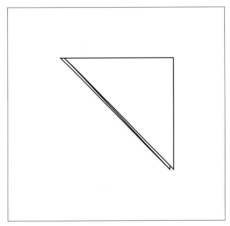

3 Fold in half again.

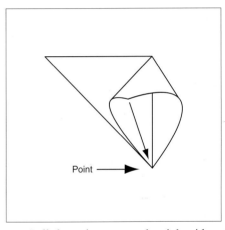

4 Pull the point over to the right side.

Point ➤

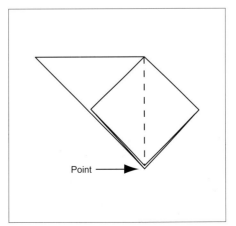

5 Bring the point down to form a square.

Point ➤

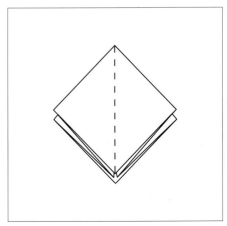

6 Turn over and repeat.

7 Fold in the two sides.

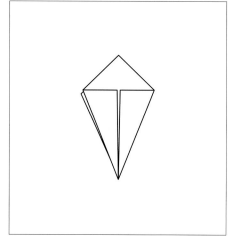

8 Turn over and repeat.

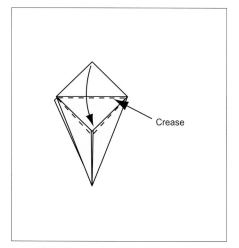

Crease

9 Fold the top down and crease, then pull back up. Turn over and repeat.

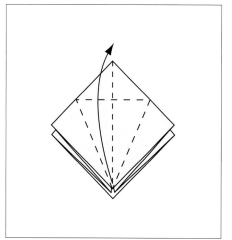

10 Open back up to form a square. Turn over and repeat.

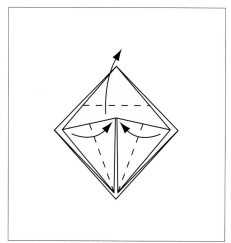

11 Pull the point of the top layer up to the crease line that was made in step 9, bringing sides to the center.

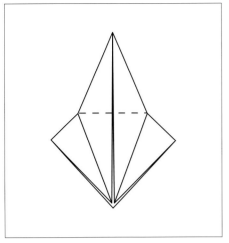

12 Crease and flatten out.

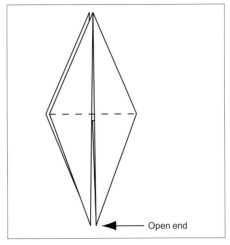

Open end

13 Turn over and repeat.

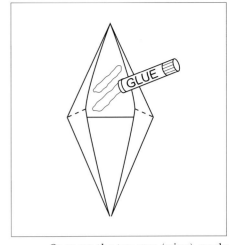

GLUE

14 Open up the top area (wing), apply glue stick, then close back up.

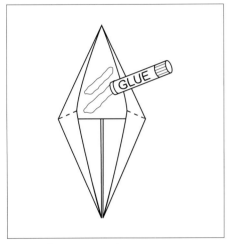

GLUE

15 Turn over and repeat.

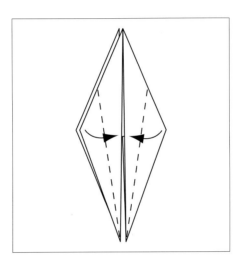

16 Fold in the two sides.

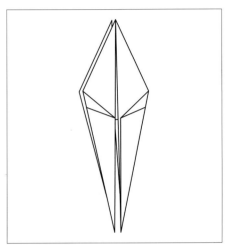

17 Turn over and repeat.

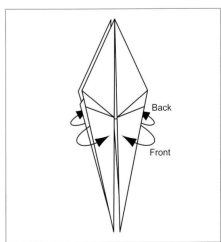

Back

Front

18 Pull in both sides on front and back.

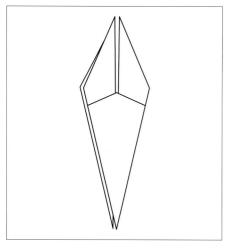

19 Turn over and repeat. The results should look like this.

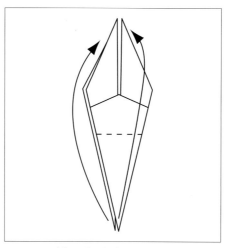

20 Fold up both front and back point sections to the crease line.

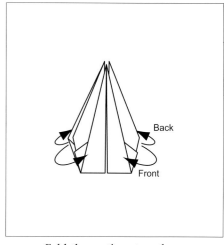

Back

Front

21 Fold the sections together on both front and back.

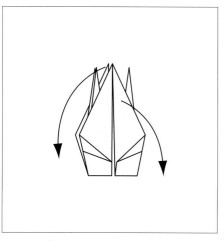

22 The results should look like this.

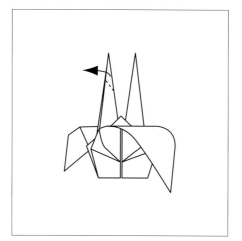

23 Pull the wings up and out. Fold down the tip on one side to form the head.

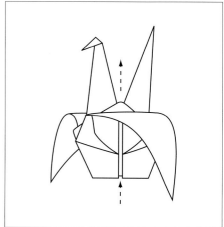

24 With the awl, enter the bottom center hole of the crane, going up through the center back.

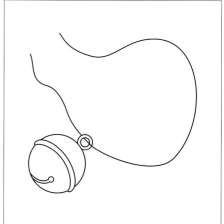

25 Pass the string through the bell loop and tie a knot.

26 Tie a bow with the gold or silver ribbon.

27 Tie the bow securely on top of the bell loop, then knot the two loose ends of the string together.

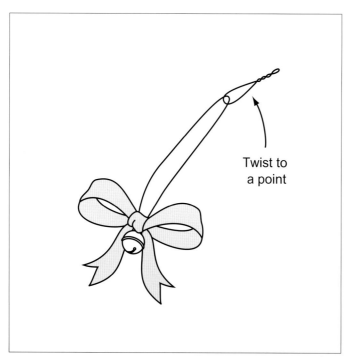

Twist to a point

28 Pull the string taught, fold the wire in half, and thread it through the string. Twist the loose ends of the wire together to form a point at the top, like a needle.

29 Insert the wire through the body of the crane and up through the hole in the center back. Put a dab of hot glue at the bottom of the crane and pull the string up so the bow sticks to the bottom. Place a dab of hot glue at the top of the crane's back to hold the string in place. Remove the wire. Use the round pencil to curve the crane's wings.

Washi-Covered Egg Ornaments

The sheer loveliness of Washi-covered eggs lends itself to any holiday, especially Christmas. Blown hen, duck, goose, and even quail eggs can be elegantly decorated to produce stunning and original ornaments for the Christmas tree. What better way to bring the themes of hope, peace, and new life to your holiday than to fill your tree with beautiful egg ornaments? Different effects can be achieved by choosing a single color theme or by combining complementary or clashing colors.

Preparing the Eggs

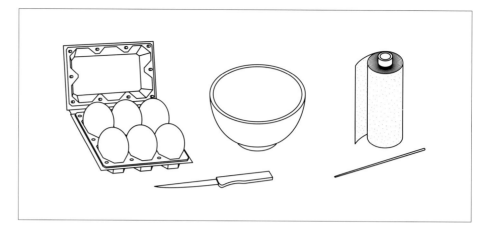

EQUIPMENT AND MATERIALS FOR SIX EGGS

- 6 hen's eggs at room temperature in a cardboard carton
- Small pointed knife
- Long toothpick or wooden skewer
- Microwave-safe dish or plate
- Paper towels

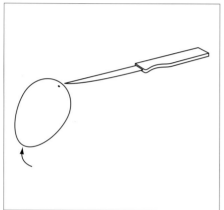

1 Carefully make a ¹/₈–¹/₄" (3–6 mm) hole at each end of one egg with the small pointed knife.

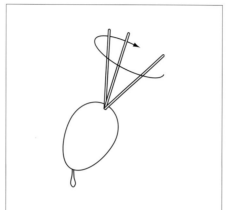

2 Insert the toothpick or skewer into one hole and gently move it around until the egg yolk is broken.

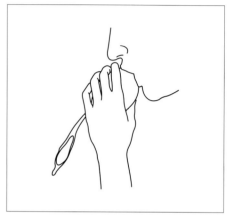

3 Blow into one hole until all the egg mixture comes out the other end. Run some water into the egg, shake it, and blow again. Repeat until the water runs clear. Repeat the process with the remaining eggs.

4 Line a microwave-safe dish with paper towels and place the eggs on the towels with one hole facing down. Microwave for 20 seconds on High. Change the paper towels and repeat. Put the eggs back into the carton and let dry for a few hours.

5 If you do not have a microwave oven, put the eggs back into the cardboard carton and wait at least a day or overnight for the eggs to dry. If water from the eggs continues to wet the carton, this indicates that the eggs are still too wet to be covered with Washi.

TIP

- The eggs must be completely dry before they are covered. If water leaks out and makes the Washi too wet, peel off the Washi and let the eggs dry out completely before re-covering them.

HEN'S EGG PATTERNS

Trace the required pattern. Lay it on the Washi and cut out the
pattern and Washi together. With practice you will be able to
cut the pattern and several layers of Washi at the same time.

Small

Large

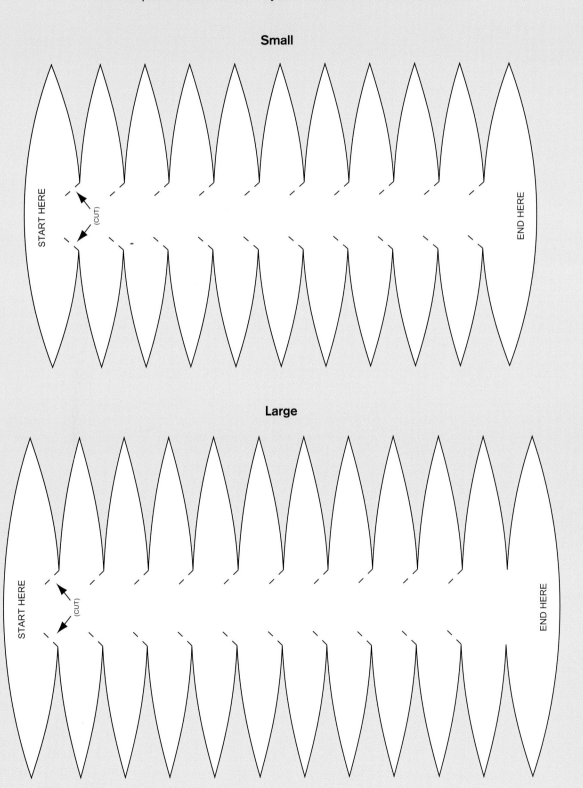

Basic Washi-Covered Eggs

EQUIPMENT AND MATERIALS

- 6 blown hen's eggs
- 1/4 sheet of printed Washi
- Small paintbrush
- White craft glue
- Tap water to mix glue
- Small cup or bowl
- Measuring tape
- Tracing paper and pencil
- Small sharp scissors
- Damp kitchen towel or washcloth
- Wooden dowel (12" x 3/8" / 30.5 x 1 cm)

6 Mix 1/4 cup of glue and 1–2 tablespoons of tap water. The glue should be easy to spread but not too watery.

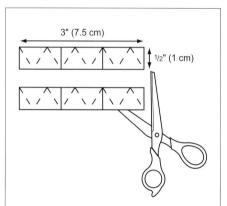

7 To reinforce the holes at each end of the egg, cut two 3" (7.5 cm) x 1/2" (1 cm) strips out of scraps of Washi. (The white borders of the Washi sheet can be used.) Cut the strips into triangles.

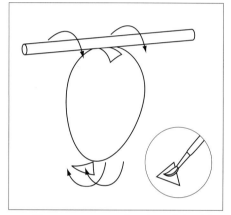

8 Glue one or two triangles, plain side up, over each hole. Cover any cracks in the eggs in the same way. Use the wooden dowel to smooth out any lumps or creases.

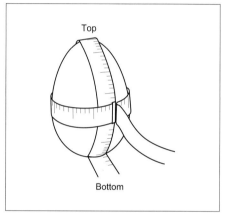

9 Measure all the eggs. One of the pattern sizes should fit the eggs, which may vary a little in size.

10 Measure the egg patterns on page 33 to see which size best fits the eggs. Trace the pattern using the tracing paper, increasing or decreasing the size as needed. Cut out the Washi.

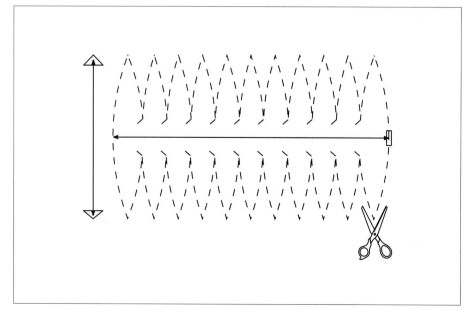

TIPS

- Always put glue on the Washi, not on the egg, and always glue one strip at a time.
- Use a damp cloth frequently to wipe any drips of glue, and to keep your hands clean.
- Do not apply too much pressure when using the dowel to smooth the Washi or the eggs will break.

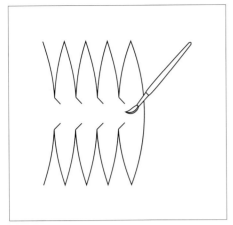

11 Brush glue on the first strip of Washi, starting at the end indicated on the pattern.

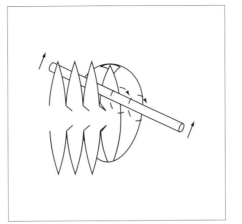

12 Center the strip, making sure that both ends reach the top (north) and bottom (south) of the egg. Roll out any lumps and creases with the wooden dowel.

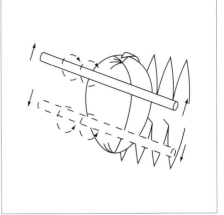

13 Continue adding strips around the egg, one at a time, making sure each piece reaches the top and bottom.

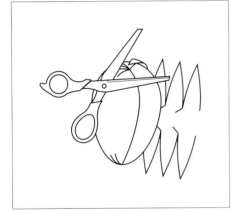

14 Halfway around the egg, start trimming the top and bottom ends of the Washi so that the points meet nicely and are centered at both ends of the egg.

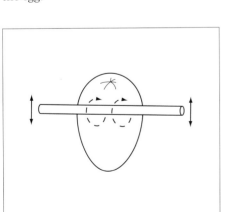

15 Use the dowel to smooth the Washi. Complete all six eggs and let them dry for one hour before adding the bead cap and cording.

Finishing the Washi-Covered Egg Ornaments

EQUIPMENT AND MATERIALS

- 6 Washi-covered eggs
- 6 bead caps (18 mm) in gold or silver, or 7½" (19 cm) of mini leaf garland
- Small wire cutter (if using leaf garland)
- 1 yard (90 cm) thin gold or silver cord cut into 6" (15 cm) lengths
- Small sharp scissors
- Hot-glue gun and glue sticks
- Cardboard egg carton
- Large piece of cardboard to protect working surface

16 Fold each 6" (15 cm) length of cord in half and knot the ends together. Pull the folded end through the hole in the bead cap, leaving the knot inside. Tie another knot if the hole is too large. (If the bead cap has a loop at the top, just thread the cording through it and then tie the knot.)

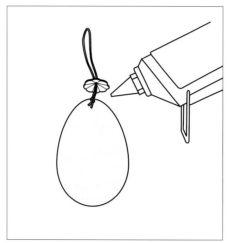

17 Put hot glue on the knotted end of the cord or inside the bead cap and quickly glue it to the narrow top of the egg.

18 If using garland, cut a 1¼" (3 cm) length of garland and twist into a circle. Fold each 6" (15 cm) length of cord in half, knot the ends together, and hot glue the knot to the top of the egg. Pull the cord through the circle of garland and hot glue the garland to the top of the egg.

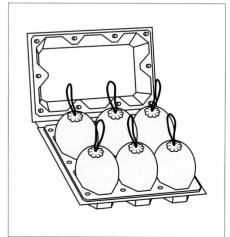

19 Place the eggs in the carton and let them dry for at least 1–2 hours before covering with shellac.

Shellacking the Washi-Covered Egg Ornaments

EQUIPMENT AND MATERIALS

- 6 Washi-covered egg ornaments
- Clothes hanger and 6 clothespins
- Large cookie sheet covered with aluminum foil to catch shellac drips
- 8-oz bottle or can of water-based shellac
- Covered container for storing the shellac
- Small paintbrush
- Small bowl large enough to dip the largest egg
- 12" (30.5 cm) cream or white cotton doily (optional)
- Tablecloth to protect working surface

TIPS

- Make sure that the Washi-covered eggs are completely dry before you begin, otherwise the Washi will peel off when the eggs are dipped into the shellac.
- Only use water-based shellac. Oil- or gas-based shellac will eat away the Washi, since it is a natural fiber.
- Pour the shellac that has dripped onto the cookie sheet back into the covered storage container so that it can be reused. Then immediately wash off the cookie sheet, as it will be very hard to clean after the shellac dries!
- A disposable foil pan or pizza pan can be used instead of a metal cookie sheet.
- Repeat the shellacking process 4–6 times to get a good shine and to strengthen the eggs.
- Let the shellacked eggs dry for 1–2 days before placing them on the tree or giving them as a gift.

20 Grasp the cord at the top of one ornament and dip the egg into the shellac.

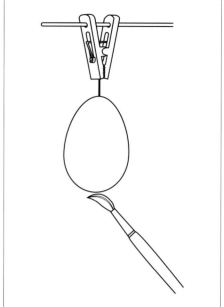

21 Clip the cord to the hanger with a clothespin. Hang up the hanger and place the cookie sheet directly below the hanger to catch any drips. Complete all six eggs, and then use the paintbrush to dab away any drips (you will have to do this 2–3 times). Let the eggs dry for at least an hour before redipping them.

22 If you prefer, hold each egg in turn and carefully brush a little shellac on one side. Place on the cotton doily, wet side up. When completely dry, shellac the other side of the eggs. Repeat 4–6 times.

Gift Box Ornament

Gifts are an essential part of everyday life, whether in Japan, America, or anywhere else in the world. The simple beauty and elegant lines of these gift boxes make them a natural for many occasions. This lovely little gift box can be made into a hanging ornament or package decoration. This is a wonderful and easy Washi craft for elementary students to do as a holiday or birthday gift.

EQUIPMENT AND MATERIALS FOR ONE GIFT BOX ORNAMENT

- 8" x 4" (20 x 10 cm) rectangle of printed Washi
- 2" x 2" (5 x 5 cm) square block of Styrofoam
- 28" x ¼" (71 cm x 6 mm) length of ribbon
- 8" (20 cm) thick gold or silver thread or thin gold or silver cording
- Miniature flowers
- Flower stamens
- Small sharp scissors
- Ruler
- Hot-glue gun and glue sticks

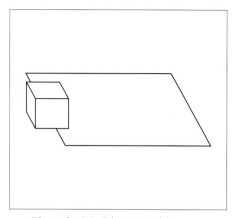

1 Place the Washi wrong side up on the table. Position the block of Styrofoam off the edge of the printed Washi at one of the narrow ends.

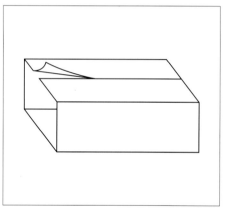

2 Roll the block over the Washi to cover it until the paper overlaps at the other end.

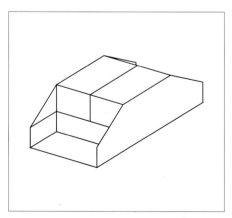

3 Following the illustration, fold in the sides, adding glue stick to keep it in place.

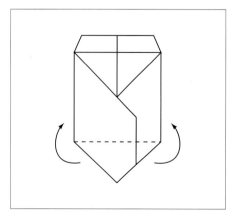

4 Continue folding in the sides as illustrated above.

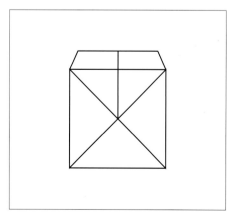

5 Both ends should meet nicely in the center, as illustrated.

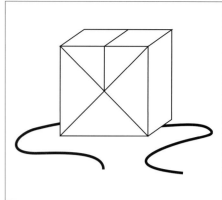

6 Place ribbon on the table and position the gift box, wrong side up, in the center.

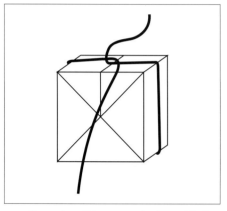

7 Cross the ribbon over itself and bring toward the opposite side. See illustration for guidance.

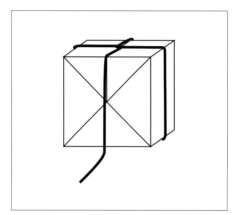

8 Flip the gift box over.

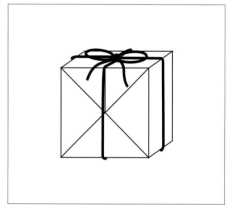

9 Tie a bow with the remaining ribbon.

10 Hot glue mini flowers and stamen under the bow.

11 To make an ornament, tie gold or silver thread or cording around the bow for hanging.

12 To make a non-hanging gift box, omit step 11. These gift boxes make festive decorations for a holiday table.

Standing Angel Decoration

1 Fold the rectangle in half length-wise. Open back up and apply glue to one side and then fold back over. Press together so it adheres nicely.

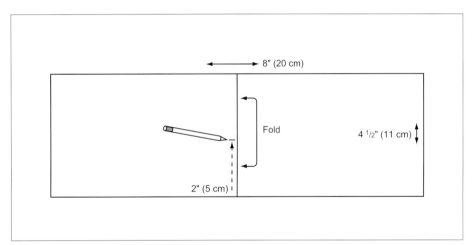

8" (20 cm)

Fold

4 1/2" (11 cm)

2" (5 cm)

2 Fold the rectangle of Washi in half lengthwise to find the center. On one side of the printed Washi, measure 2" (5 cm) up the center fold and mark with a pencil.

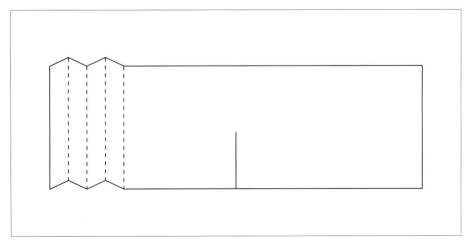

3 Starting at one 4¹/₂" (11.5 cm) end, accordion fold (fan fold) into approximately ³/₈" (1 cm) folds, all the way to the other end.

A ngels have always played a special role in the hearts of people around the world, especially during the holiday season. The angelic symbolism of peace, hope, and protection makes angels a natural for Washi crafts. The vast array of Washi colors and patterns means that angels of immense color and beauty can be easily created by all ages. Angels will add spice and character to any setting or decor.

EQUIPMENT AND MATERIALS FOR ONE ANGEL

- One 8" x 9" (20 x 23 cm) rectangle of printed Washi
- 10 mm painted wooden head bead with large 1/4" (6 mm) holes (or paint a face on a plain wooden bead)
- 2" (5 cm) gold or silver tinsel chenille stem
- 4" (10 cm) gold or silver tinsel chenille stem for halo
- Tiny bow or flower (optional)
- 2" (5 cm) Styrofoam ball for the stand
- 3¹/₂" x 3¹/₂" (9 x 9 cm) square of ¹/₈" (3mm) batting to cover the stand
- 8" (20 cm) decorative cording (¹/₄" / 6mm diameter) for the bottom of the stand
- Wooden toothpick
- Straight pin
- Small sharp scissors
- Tracing paper, pencil, and ruler
- Glue stick or craft paste
- Hot-glue gun and glue sticks
- Sharp cutting blade

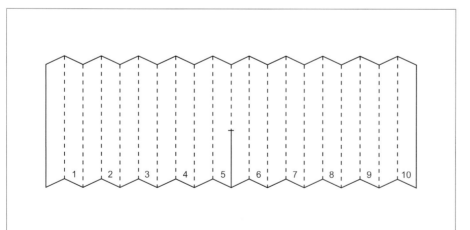

4 When completed there should be 10–12 ridges on the front side (5–6 on either side of the center fold). Size will vary depending on the size of the folds. Find the pencil mark and cut 2" (5 cm) up to the mark of the center fold. Before you cut, make sure there are the same number of folds on either side of the center fold. If not, move to another fold to even the folds on each side. Alternatively, your angel can have short wings or the wings can be a full circle. For short wings, make the cut 1½" (4 cm) long; for full-circle wings, cut 2½" (6 cm).

5 Bend the 4" (10 cm) tinsel chenille stem to form a small halo at one end and pull the other end through the wooden bead head.

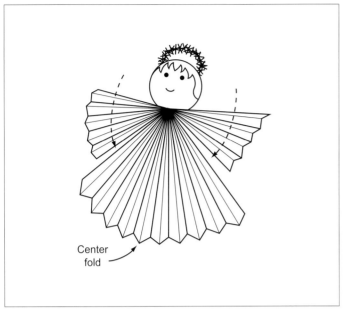

Center fold

6 Fold the wings down on either side of the angel. Put glue all the way down the inside center fold, on the front side. Glue the chenille stem extending from the neck in between the front center fold. Place a dab of hot glue on the toothpick, then place it below the chenille stem, with the pointed end extending ¹/₂" (1 cm) from the angel's hem.

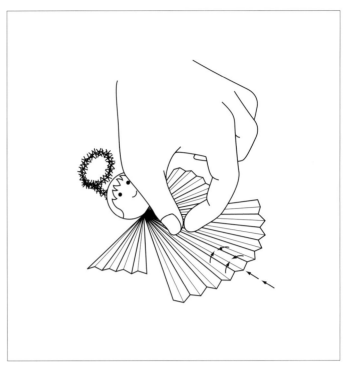

7 Quickly pinch the seams together to conceal the chenille stem and the toothpick; hold for a few seconds.

8 Starting from the front of the angel and passing toward the back, pull and twist the 2" (5 cm) chenille stem securely to the back of the angel. You may need to trim off some excess chenille stem. Alternatively, you can tie the chenille stem toward the front and use it as arms to hold a small folded piece of paper that looks like a hymnal.

Pull, twist

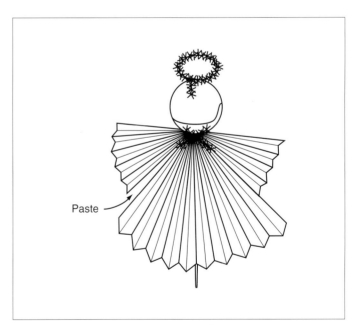

Paste

9 Glue the inside of the wings to the dress.

10 If desired, hot glue a tiny bow or flower under the angel's neck at the front. If you placed the arms in front, cut a piece of white paper 1¹/₂" x ³/₄" (4 x 2 cm), fold in half widthwise, and hot glue to the angel's arms. (Refer to finished photo on page 44 for guidance.)

Preparing the Decorative Angel Stand

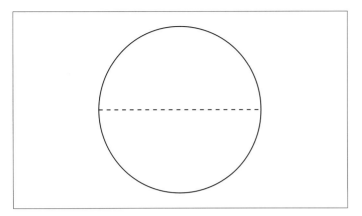

11 Cut the 2" (5 cm) Styrofoam ball in half, using the sharp cutting blade. You will only need half for the stand; save the other half for another angel.

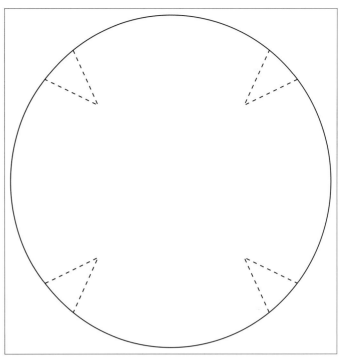

12 Trace the fiberfill pattern above. Use it to cut out the batting. Cut off the four triangles as indicated.

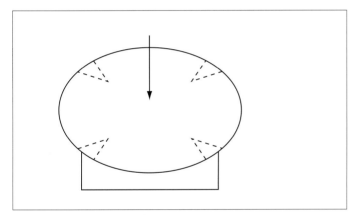

13 With the straight pin, pin the center of the circle of batting to the center top of the Styrofoam. Run hot glue along the bottom edge of a quarter of the Styrofoam circle and quickly pull the batting down over the hot glue. Hold for a second, then do the opposite side. Continue with the other two sides.

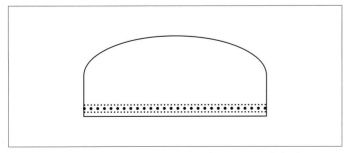

14 Trim off all the excess batting from around the bottom edges so the stand will sit nicely on a flat surface. Carefully hot glue the decorative cording all around the bottom of the stand. Trim off any excess cording.

15 Finish off your angel by inserting the tip of the toothpick into the center of the stand.

Holiday Wreaths

Wreaths displayed throughout the seasons are a nice way to welcome guests to your home or office. Adding Washi ornaments will bring new meaning to your wreaths. The Christmas season is an especially great time to display a lovely Washi wreath, but you can use different colors to suit other seasons, too.

EQUIPMENT AND MATERIALS FOR ONE WREATH

- Purchased loose wicker or vine wreath (12" or 6" / 30.5 or 15 cm diameter)
- Printed or solid Washi squares (4" x 4" / 10 x 10 cm), 24 for larger wreath or 12 for smaller wreath
- Package of (12" / 30.5 cm) covered florist stem wires (24 for larger wreath or 12 for smaller wreath)
- Tracing paper and pencil
- Small sharp scissors
- Ruler or measuring tape
- Glue stick
- Awl (optional)
- Paper clip

1 Trace the pattern of your choice from page 52.

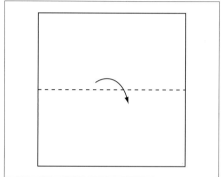

2 Fold a 4" x 4" (10 x 10 cm) square of Washi in half. Open back up, apply glue stick to one side, and then fold back over.

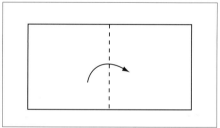

3 Fold the piece of Washi in half again, paper clip the pattern to it and cut out. You should have two patterns cut out. Repeat steps 2–3 with remaining pieces of Washi.

ASSORTED WREATH PATTERN SHAPES

Copy the pattern using tracing paper and a pencil.

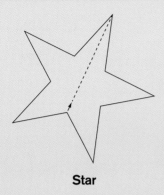

Star

Poinsettia

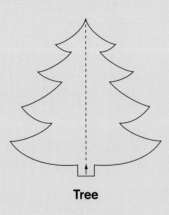

Tree

Bird

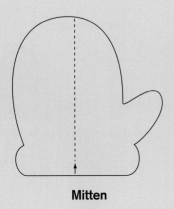

Mitten

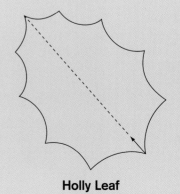

Holly Leaf

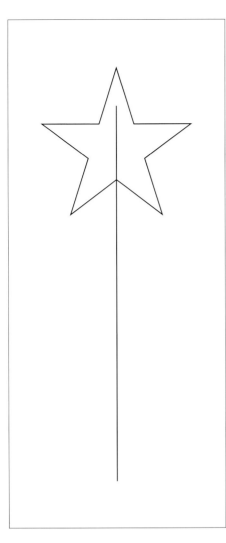

4 Carefully open up the indicated Washi ends on the pattern. Insert the florist wire into the opening and push the wire down the middle, nearly to the other end. Close back up and press together and let it completely dry before using. You can also use the awl to make decorative creases on the different shapes for a three-dimensional look.

6 Twist the loose end of the florist wire around the pencil to curl the wire into vinelike tendrils.

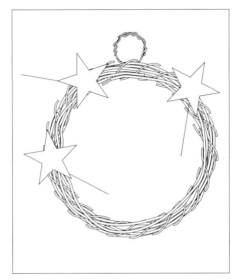

5 Insert the florist stem through the loose wicker or vines on the wreath until the shape touches the wreath. Twist the wire to secure it to the wreath.

NOTE

Add a Washi Angel, Poinsettia, Star, or any other Christmas ornament to the top or center of your holiday wreath to celebrate the season.

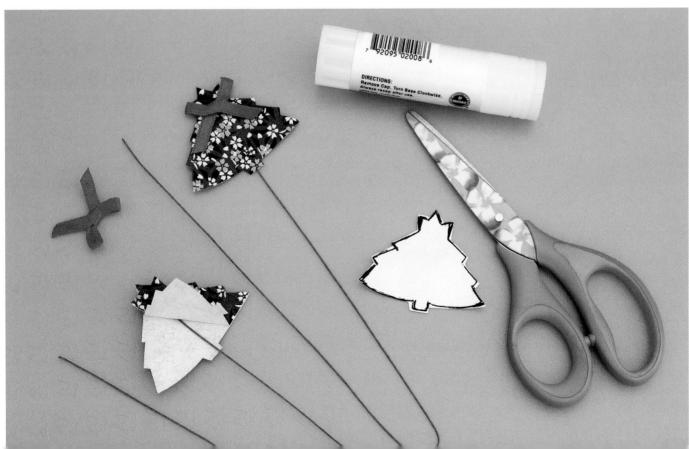

Star Ornament

L et the beautiful Christmas Washi Star shine as a holiday table centerpiece, a hanging tree ornament, or a tree top-per. The colorful Washi stars are a different way to add to the special celebrations during the holiday season. The wonderful colors will add elegance to any special Christmas dinner.

EQUIPMENT AND MATERIALS FOR ONE STAR ORNAMENT

- 6¹/2" x 6¹/2" (16.5 x 16.5 cm) square of printed Washi for pattern A
- 6" x 6" (15 x 15 cm) square of printed Washi for pattern B
- Two 6" x 6" (15 x 15 cm) squares of tag board for patterns C and D
- 8" (20 cm) of thin gold or silver cording
- Tracing paper and pencil
- Tape
- Paper clips
- Small sharp scissors
- Ruler
- Hot-glue gun and glue sticks

If you are making the star on a stick:
- 8" or 12" (20 or 30.5 cm) bamboo skewer
- Thick-pointed red, green, or blue felt tipped marker

If you are making the star with decorative cording:
- 24" (61 cm) decorative cording (¹/4" / 6mm diameter)
- ¹/2" (1 cm) round bells (optional)

Star Side (A)
Printed Washi Pattern
Cut one (1)

1 Trace the patterns and cut out printed Washi.

Star Side (B)
Printed Washi Pattern
Cut one (1)

Star Side (C & D)
Tag Board Pattern
Cut two (2)

2 Trace the pattern and cut out tag board.

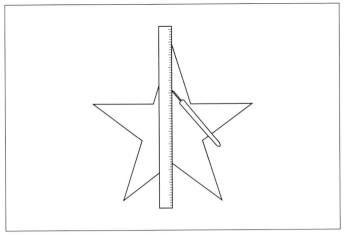

3 Using the awl and ruler, score from each point to the opposite of star sides C and D. See illustration for guidance.

4 When you have made all 5 scores, fold to crease all the segments (from the points to the center) outward and the short segments inward. This will cause the center of the star to push up and out.

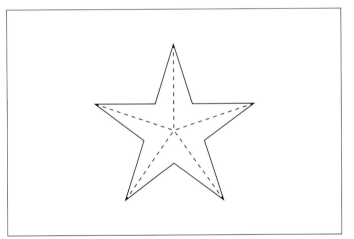

5 Tape all around side C to side D, securing them together; leave one star point unsecured.

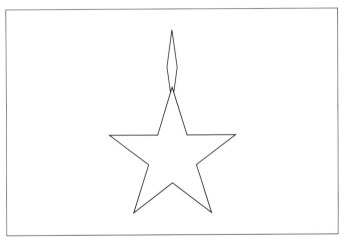

6 Fold the 8" (20 cm) cording in half and then knot the loose ends together. Tape the knotted side securely to the unsecured star point of side D. Tape the other piece of side C to side D, thus completing the star.

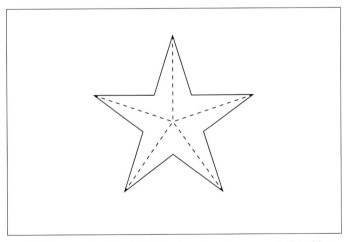

7 Fold cut-out printed Washi piece A and crease all the sides like you did tag board sides C and D.

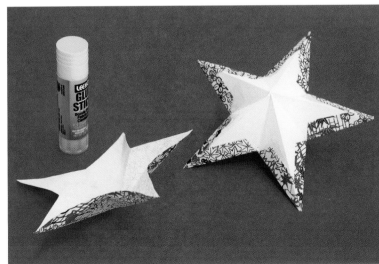

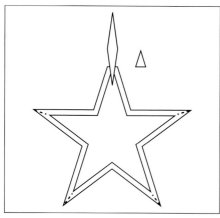

8 Apply glue to the wrong side of printed Washi pattern piece A and match it up with one side of the completed star. Smooth out the printed Washi. Snip off the top triangle piece where the cording is, then snip in five corners. See illustration for guidance.

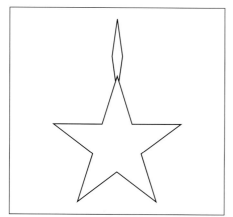

9 Paste all the extending edges over to the other side. Trim off the extra Washi at the points.

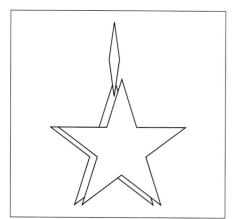

10 Glue printed Washi B on the unfinished side of the star and smooth out. If any Washi sticks out around the star, snip it off. Let the star completely dry before placing on the tree.

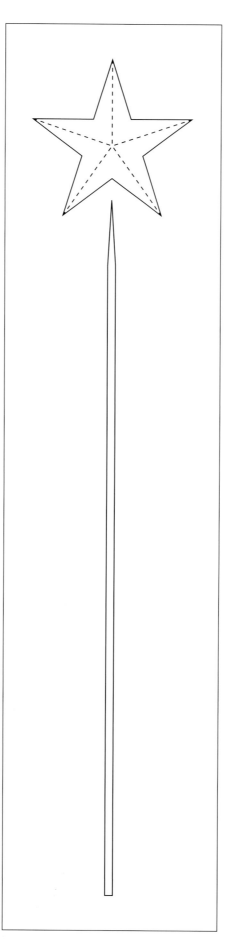

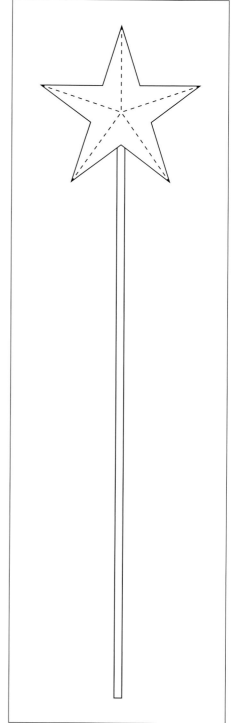

11 For a star on a stick you may decide to keep the cording or string at the top of the star and fray it for decoration. Use a thick-pointed red, green or blue felt-tipped maker to color the wooden skewer. Poke a hole with the awl in the end of the star opposite from the cording. Add a dab of hot glue and insert the pointed end of the skewer. Let it dry for a few minutes to secure the skewer to the star.

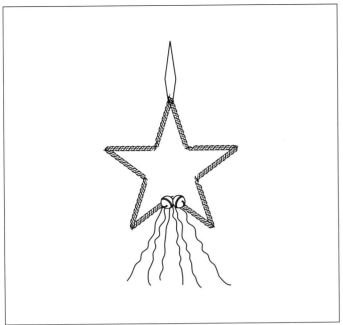

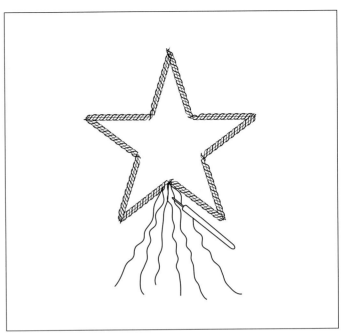

12 Add a little holiday flair to your Washi Star ornaments or tree toppers with decorative cording. Fold the decorative cording in half. Start by hot gluing the center halfway point of the decorative cording on one of the star tips. Then hot glue the rest of the cording down the right-hand side of the star, then the left-hand side. Make sure both cords meet at the center angle. See illustration for additional guidance. The remainder of the cording can be spread apart and frayed. To add the two round bells, tie two strands of the frayed cording to the bells. Add a dab of hot glue on each knot to secure the bell to the cord.

13 For a tree topper, with the awl, make a 1/4" (6 mm) hole (or large enough so that the top of your tree will fit in it). The remainder of the cording can be spread apart and frayed and the bells added. If you want longer frayed cording on the top of the tree, use longer, thicker cording.

Washi-Covered Glass Ornaments

Discover the eloquence of turning old ornaments into Washi treasures. Covering plain glass ornaments with beautiful Washi is a holiday delight that will fill your home with the richness of the many colors of Washi while extending the life of the ornaments. This conversation piece will inspire your friends to do the same with their old glass ornaments.

EQUIPMENT AND MATERIALS FOR SIX ORNAMENTS

- Six 2¼" (5.5 cm) or 2⅝" (6.5 cm) or eight 1¾" (4 cm) glass ornaments
- ¼ sheet of printed Washi
- Gold spray paint (optional)
- Small paintbrush
- White craft glue
- Tap water
- Small cup or bowl for mixing glue
- Measuring tape
- Tracing paper and pencil
- Small sharp scissors
- Damp kitchen towel or washcloth
- Wooden dowel (12" long x ⅜" / 30.5 x 1 cm)

TIPS

- Don't throw away any old Christmas ornaments! Buy new ones only after the holidays when they go on sale, or pick them up at flea markets for very little money.
- To prevent the ornament color from showing through the design of the Washi, it is best to cover a red ornament with printed Washi that has a red base, a blue ornament with blue-base printed Washi, and so on. Gold or silver ornaments can be covered using any color of printed Washi.

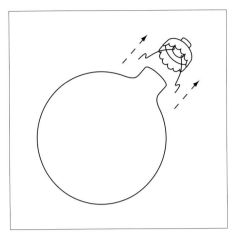

1 Carefully remove the wires and caps from the ornaments. If desired, spray paint the caps and wires gold.

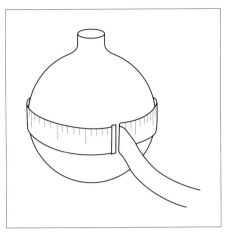

2 Measure your glass ornaments.

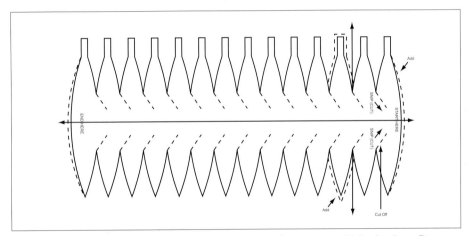

3 Measure the ornament patterns on pages 65 and 66 to see which size best fits your ornaments. Trace the pattern using the tracing paper, increasing or decreasing the size as needed.

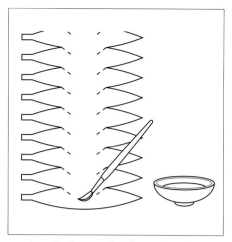

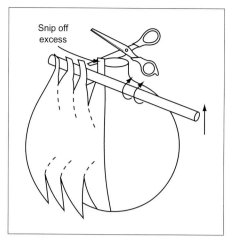

5 Brush glue on the first strip of Washi, starting at the end indicated on the pattern.

6 Center the strip, making sure that the correct ends reach the top and bottom of the ornament. Use the dowel to roll out any lumps and creases on each strip.

TIPS

- Always put the glue on the Washi, not on the ornament, and always glue one strip at a time.

- Use a damp cloth frequently to wipe any drips of glue, and to keep your hands clean.

- Do not apply too much pressure when using the dowel to smooth the Washi or the ornament will break.

ORNAMENT PATTERNS

Trace the required pattern. Lay it on the Washi and cut out the
pattern and Washi together. With practice, you will be able to
cut the pattern and several layers of Washi at the same time.

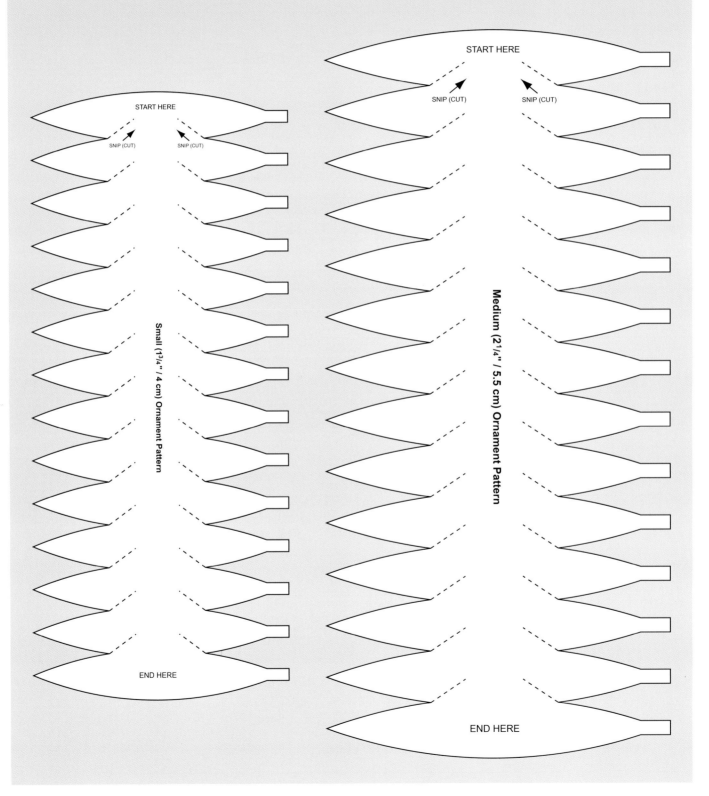

LARGE ORNAMENT PATTERN

Trace the required pattern. Lay it on the Washi and cut out the pattern and Washi together.
With practice, you will be able to cut the pattern and several layers of Washi at the same time.

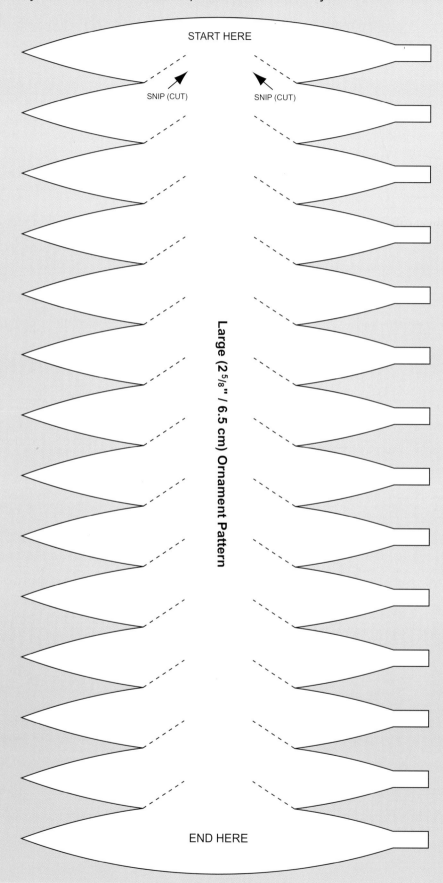

START HERE

SNIP (CUT)   SNIP (CUT)

Large (2⁵/₈" / 6.5 cm) Ornament Pattern

END HERE

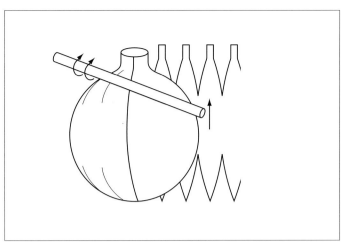

7 Continue around the ornament, one segment at a time, using the dowel to roll out any lumps and creases.

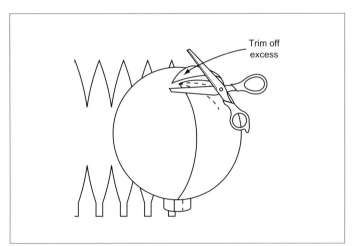

Trim off excess

8 Halfway around the ornament, start trimming the excess Washi at the bottom of the ornament, so that all points meet nicely in the center.

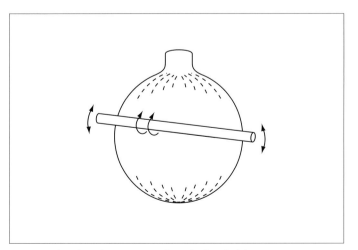

9 Use the dowel to go over the whole Washi ornaments to make sure that there are no lumps or creases. Complete all ornaments and let dry for 4–6 hours before shellacking them.

Shellacking the Washi-Covered Glass Ornaments

EQUIPMENT AND MATERIALS

- 6 completely dried Washi-covered ornaments
- Clothes hanger and 6 clothespins
- Large cookie sheet covered with aluminum foil to catch shellac drips
- 8-oz bottle or can of water-based shellac
- Covered container for storing the shellac
- Small paintbrush
- Small deep bowl large enough to dip the largest ornament

TIPS

- Make sure your Washi-covered ornaments are completely dry before you begin, otherwise the Washi will peel off when the ornaments are dipped into the shellac. Average drying time is from 4–6 hours.
- Use only water-based shellac. Oil- or gas-based shellac will eat away the Washi, since it is a natural fiber.
- Pour enough shellac in the bowl so that it completely covers the largest ornament you are shellacking.
- Pour the shellac that has dripped onto the cookie sheet back into the covered storage container so that it can be reused. Then immediately wash off the cookie sheet, as it will be very hard to clean after the shellac dries!
- A disposable foil pan or pizza pan can be used instead of a metal cookie sheet.
- Repeat the shellacking process 4–6 times to get a good shine and to strengthen the ornaments.
- Let the shellacked ornaments dry for 1–2 days before hanging on the tree.

10 Put all the caps and wires back on the ornaments.

11 Holding the ornament by the wire, carefully dip the ornament into the bowl of shellac. Push the ornament down so it does not float.

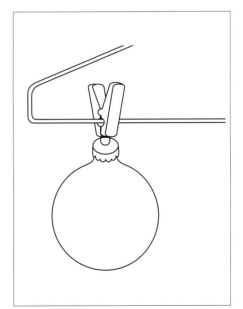

12 Hang up the hanger and place the cookie sheet directly below the hanger to catch any drips. After dipping an ornament, clip it to the hanger with a clothespin.

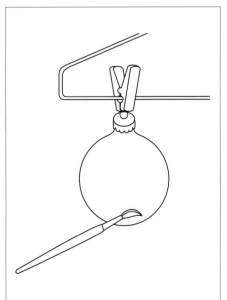

13 After you have dipped and clipped all the ornaments to the hanger, use the paintbrush to dab away any drips (you will have to do this 2–3 times). When the ornaments no longer drip, let them dry for at least 1–2 hours before shellacking them again.

Spicing Up Your Washi-Covered Glass Ornaments

EQUIPMENT AND MATERIALS

- 6 completely dried Washi-covered and shellacked ornaments
- 2–3 dozen mini flowers (such as ribbon roses)
- 2 yards (2 meters) narrow satin ribbon to match the printed Washi
- Small wire cutters (if flower wires are too thick to cut with scissors)
- Small sharp scissors
- Hot-glue gun and glue sticks

TIP
- Remember that there is really no correct way to place the bows and mini flowers on the ornaments. Follow these examples and then be creative and try different ways to decorate your own ornaments.

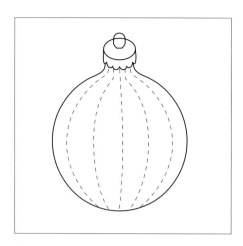

14 When the ornaments are covered, shellacked, and completely dry with the caps and wires back, they are ready to be decorated.

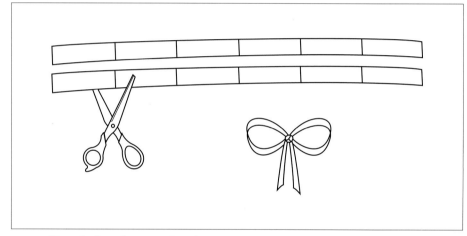

15 Heat the hot-glue gun. Cut the ribbon into 6" (15 cm) lengths. Tie each length into a small bow.

16 Hot glue a bow on either side of the cap.

17 Carefully snip the wires off the mini flowers. Hot glue the mini flowers around, on top, and in between the bows. You can also hot glue some bows and flowers to the bottom of the ornament. This is especially useful if you did not get all the shellac drips!

Poinsettia Centerpiece

Flowers speak of caring, love, and friendship, adding a rich ambiance to any setting. They serve as wonderful gifts any time of the year, but especially during the holidays. This elegant Poinsettia centerpiece will serve many gift purposes, table settings, and home or office displays. You may want to venture beyond the traditional Christmas colors and create your own flowers with printed Washi in colors to suit your holiday decor. The possibilities are limitless.

EQUIPMENT AND MATERIALS FOR ONE POINSETTIA

- 8" x 6 1/2" (20 x 16.5 cm) rectangle of printed Washi for the large petals
- 6 1/2" x 5 1/2" (16.5 x 14 cm) rectangle of printed Washi for the medium petals
- 5 1/2" x 5" (14 x 12.5 cm) rectangle of printed Washi for the small petals
- 10 1/2" x 7" (26.5 x 17.5 cm) rectangle of solid Washi for the leaves
- 5 extra large gold/silver/yellow single-ended flower bulb centers or stamens
- 10 covered florist stem wire (12" / 30.5 cm), each cut into two 6" (15 cm) pieces
- Small wire cutters
- Roll of green florist tape
- Paper clips
- Small sharp scissors
- Tracing paper, ruler, and pencil
- Glue stick

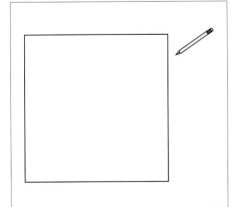

1 Trace the petal and leaf patterns on page 75.

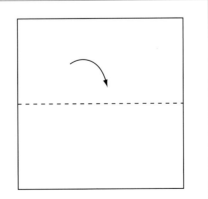

2 Fold one of the printed Washi rectangles in half and crease. Open it back up, apply glue stick to one half, then fold in half again and press to secure.

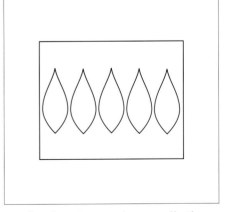

3 Starting at one end, paper clip the glued piece of Washi to the corresponding Washi pattern and cut out. Repeat until you have five petals.

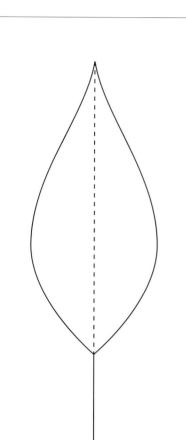

5 Twist together the wires of the five large flower bulbs or stamens. Wrap the flower center with some florist tape.

6 Grasp the flower center and start adding the printed Washi petals to the flower center, beginning with the five small ones. Place the five petals around the base of the flower center and wrap tightly with florist tape to secure the petals to the center. Continue with the next five medium ones, then the next five large ones.

4 Carefully open up the indicated Washi ends on the illustrated pattern. Insert one end of the florist wire into the opening and push the wire down the middle, nearly to the other end. Close back up and press together. Cut out and wire the rest of the petals and leaves—5 of each.

IMPORTANT

Glue and cut out each rectangle piece of Washi separately, since the glue could dry and it will be too hard to open up each petal to insert the florist wire. When you have completed all the petals and leaves, put them aside to dry as you prepare the flower center.

POINSETTIA PETAL/LEAF PATTERNS

Copy the pattern using tracing paper and a pencil.

Large Poinsettia Printed Washi Petal Pattern

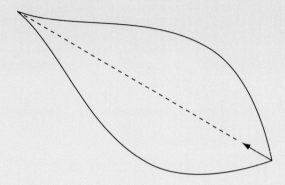

Medium Poinsettia Printed Washi Petal Pattern

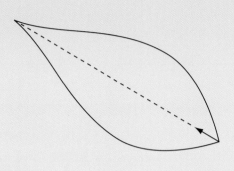

Small Poinsettia Printed Washi Petal Pattern

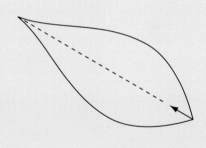

Solid Washi Poinsettia Leaf Pattern

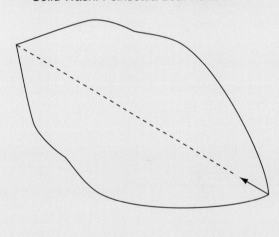

7 Complete the Poinsettia with the five solid Washi leaves, twisting the florist tape underneath the flower to secure them. Continue down, stretching and winding the tape until all of the wires are completely covered. When you reach the bottom of the wires, go under the end tip, then twist back up about 2" (5 cm). You will need to spread and even out the petals and leaves.

For a Poinsettia centerpiece, make one flower and place it in the container you wish to use. This will give you an idea of how many additional flowers you will need to make.

January 2007

Mon	Tue	Wed	Thu	Fri	Sat	Sun
1	2	3	4	5	6	7
8	9	10	11	12	13	14
15	16	17	18	19	20	21
22	23	24	25	26	27	28
29	30	31				

February 2007

Mon	Tue	Wed	Thu	Fri	Sat	Sun
			1	2	3	4
5	6	7	8	9	10	11
12	13	14	15	16	17	18
19	20	21	22	23	24	25
26	27	28				

Refrigerator Calendar Magnet

This delightful little calendar is very easy to make. Design one to follow the calendar year, the fiscal year, or the school year. Or make one showing just the 25 days leading up to Christmas to help small children to look forward to Christmas Day!

EQUIPMENT AND MATERIALS FOR ONE CALENDAR

- Printed Washi rectangle—11" x 4$^{1}/_{4}$" (28 x 10.5 cm) for large calendar, or 5$^{1}/_{2}$" x 4$^{1}/_{4}$" (14 x 10.5 cm) for small calendar
- Solid Washi rectangle—9$^{1}/_{4}$" x 2$^{1}/_{2}$" (23.5 x 6 cm) for large, 4$^{5}/_{8}$" x 2$^{1}/_{4}$" (11.5 x 5.5 cm) for small
- Rectangle of $^{1}/_{4}$" (6 mm) thick cardboard—9$^{1}/_{2}$" x 2$^{3}/_{4}$" (24 x 7 cm) for large, or 4$^{3}/_{4}$" x 2$^{3}/_{4}$" (12 x 7 cm) for small
- Magnetic strips (2$^{1}/_{4}$" x $^{1}/_{2}$" / 5.5 x 1 cm)—3 strips for large, or 2 strips for small
- Miniature flowers, small bows, and cutout designs (optional)
- Computer with calendar program (optional)
- Small sharp scissors
- Glue stick
- Ruler
- Mini stapler
- Hot-glue gun and glue sticks

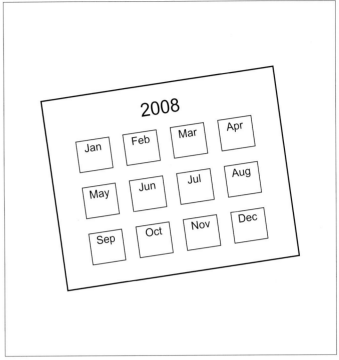

1 Print out a small yearly calendar on a computer or photocopy the sample calendar pages on page 81.

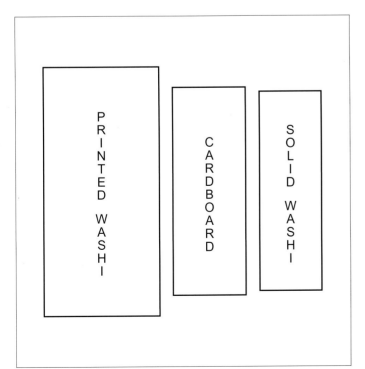

2 Once you decide which size calendar you would like to make, cut out the appropriate pieces of Washi and cardboard.

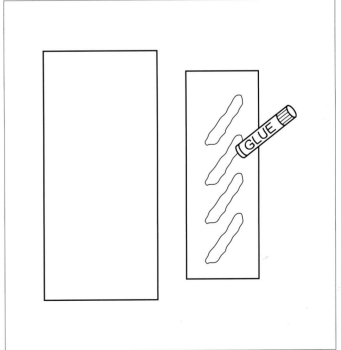

3 Place the rectangle of printed Washi on the table, wrong side up. Spread glue stick on one side of the cardboard.

January 2007						
Mon	Tue	Wed	Thu	Fri	Sat	Sun
1	2	3	4	5	6	7
8	9	10	11	12	13	14
15	16	17	18	19	20	21
22	23	24	25	26	27	28
29	30	31				

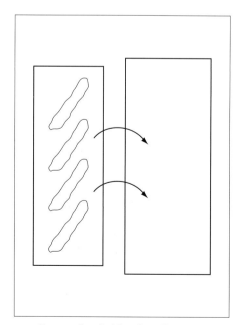

4 Center glued side of cardboard in the center of the Washi, then turn over and smooth out the Washi.

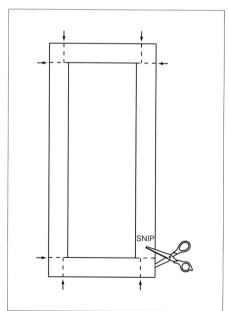

SNIP

5 Place back on the table and snip (cut) all the areas indicated in the illustration.

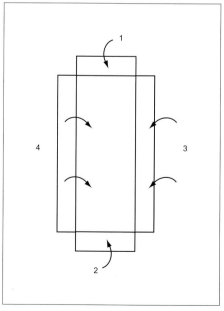

6 Apply glue to all extending sections and fold over the cardboard in the order shown in the illustration. Smooth down the sections.

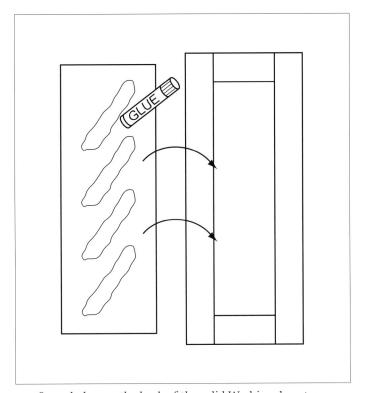

7 Spread glue on the back of the solid Washi and center the solid piece of Washi over the exposed cardboard. Smooth out. If any pieces of Washi extend out past the edge, just snip them off.

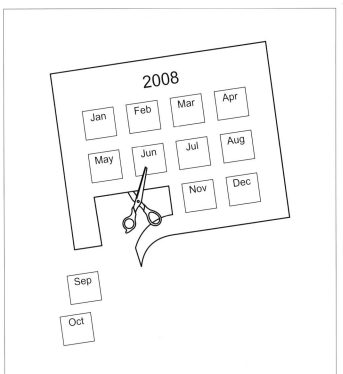

8 Cut out the calendar squares/rectangles. If you are making the large size, divide the months into three stacks. For the small calendar there will be only one stack.

9 Staple the stack(s) at the top with the mini stapler. Decide where to place your calendar stack(s) on the Washi-covered cardboard. (Be sure to leave enough room at the top for your decoration.) Spread glue on the back of each stack and place. Press down and hold for a few minutes so that the glue adheres.

10 If desired, hot glue mini flowers and a bow at the top. Or add a small fan or crane for decoration.

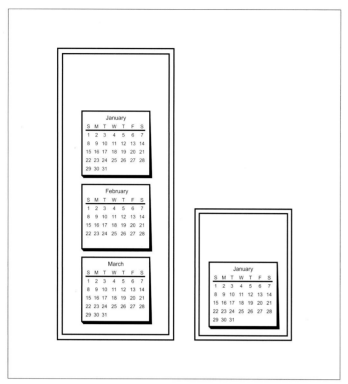

11 If you prefer Washi cutout designs, glue them at the top.

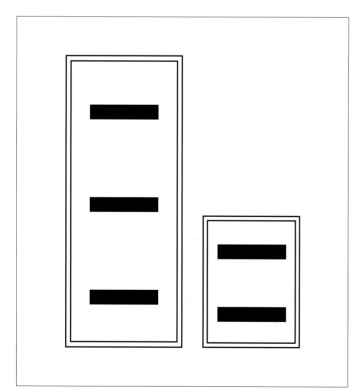

12 Glue magnet strips to the back of the calendar.

January

Mon	Tue	Wed	Thu	Fri	Sat	Sun

February

Mon	Tue	Wed	Thu	Fri	Sat	Sun

March

Mon	Tue	Wed	Thu	Fri	Sat	Sun

April

Mon	Tue	Wed	Thu	Fri	Sat	Sun

May

Mon	Tue	Wed	Thu	Fri	Sat	Sun

June

Mon	Tue	Wed	Thu	Fri	Sat	Sun

July

Mon	Tue	Wed	Thu	Fri	Sat	Sun

August

Mon	Tue	Wed	Thu	Fri	Sat	Sun

September

Mon	Tue	Wed	Thu	Fri	Sat	Sun

October

Mon	Tue	Wed	Thu	Fri	Sat	Sun

November

Mon	Tue	Wed	Thu	Fri	Sat	Sun

December

Mon	Tue	Wed	Thu	Fri	Sat	Sun

Photo Album

Give your next photo album an Asian touch by covering it with Washi, a fast and easy way to spruce up a new or old photo album. This personal and unique touch will thrill the receiver with a lasting lifetime gift.

EQUIPMENT AND MATERIALS FOR ONE PHOTO ALBUM

- $\frac{1}{2}$ sheet (19$\frac{1}{2}$" x 13" / 50 x 33 cm) of printed Washi
- $\frac{1}{2}$ sheet (19$\frac{1}{2}$" x 13" / 50 x 33 cm) of solid Washi
- $\frac{1}{2}$ sheet (19$\frac{1}{2}$" x 13" / 50 x 33 cm) of designed printed Washi
- Photo album (the kind that can be taken apart)
- Small screwdriver
- Small sharp scissors
- Pencil
- Ruler
- Glue stick
- Awl
- Medium sandpaper

TIP

- You can cut out a centerpiece for the front of the photo album from the designed Washi that you will be using.

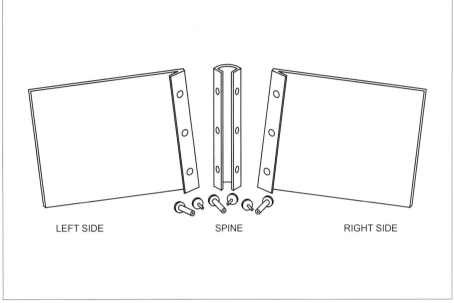

LEFT SIDE   SPINE   RIGHT SIDE

1 Take the photo album apart using a small screwdriver.

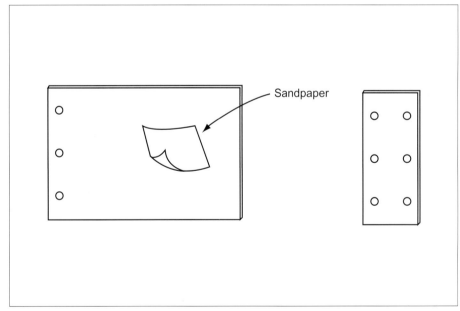

Sandpaper

2 Use sandpaper to roughen up the outside and inside edges of the photo album. Most photo albums have a smooth laminated covering to which glue does not adhere very well. Sanding the surface gives it some "tooth" so the glue and Washi will adhere better and stay attached.

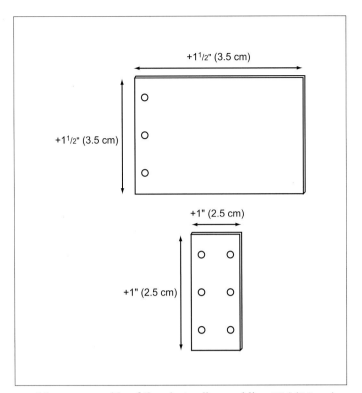

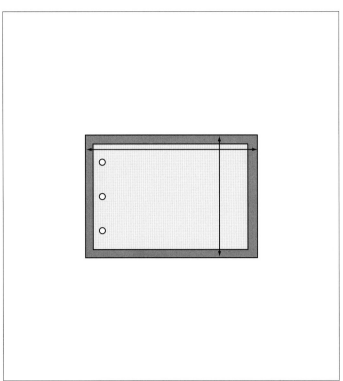

3 Measure one side of the photo album adding 1¹/₂" (3.5 cm) to the height and the length. Cut two pieces of printed Washi, one for the front and one for the back. Measure the spine and add 1" (2.5 cm) to the height and the length. Cut one piece of printed Washi.

4 Measure the inside of the photo album and subtract ¹/₂" (1 cm) from the height and length. Cut two pieces of solid Washi for the insides of the album.

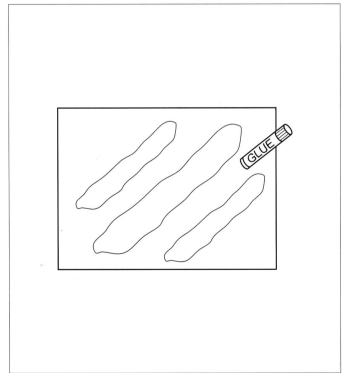

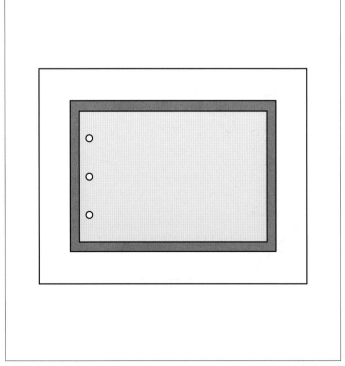

5 Place one of the large pieces of printed Washi wrong side up on the table. Spread glue all over the piece of Washi.

6 Center the right side of the photo album on the glued Washi. Carefully turn over and smooth out any lumps in the Washi.

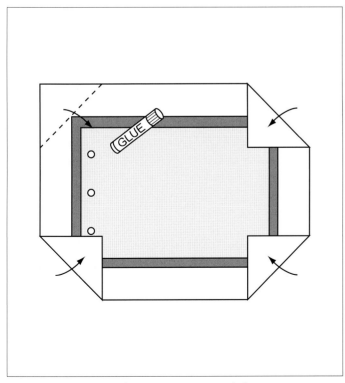

7 Fold all four Washi corners over toward the center.

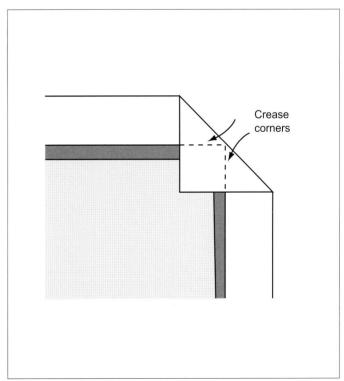

8 Crease the edges in on all the corners.

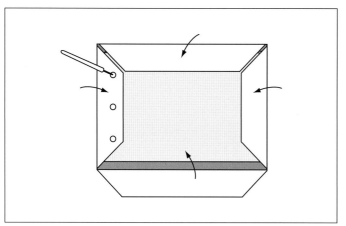

9 Feel through the Washi to find the side screw holes that hold the album together. With the awl, poke corresponding holes in the Washi. Fold the four sides over toward the center.

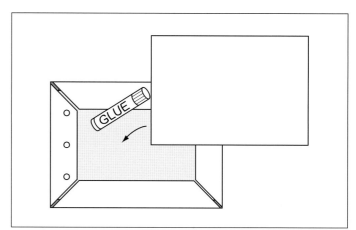

10 Put glue on the inside of the album and place the solid piece of Washi on top. Repeat steps 5–9 with the other side of the photo album.

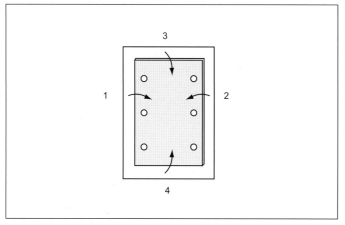

11 Spread glue on the wrong side of the center piece of Washi. Place the spine on the Washi and fold the sides up in the order shown in the illustration. Smooth out the Washi. Put all three pieces of the album aside to dry completely.

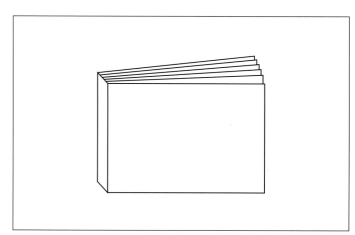

12 After the album is dry, assemble it back together.

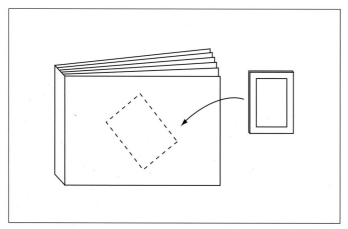

13 Decide on a design made up of squares or rectangles to glue on the front cover of the album. First glue all of the separate pieces together, then glue this on top of the album cover.

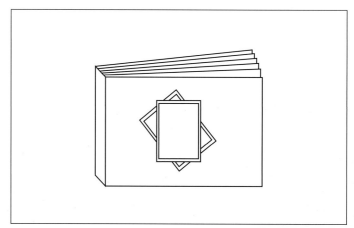

14 Glue the centerpiece cut out of the designed Washi piece on top. Let the album dry completely for 4 hours or more.

Basic Gift-Box Wrapping

Gifts add so much to people's lives all over the world. The elegant lines of these easy-to-wrap gift boxes will transform any gift into the perfect one.

EQUIPMENT AND MATERIALS FOR ONE GIFT BOX AND ONE DECORATION

- Gift box ready to be wrapped
- Printed Washi (to fit the size of box)
- Ruler or measuring tape
- Pencil and paper
- Sharp scissors
- Tape
- Hot-glue gun and glue sticks (optional)
- 1/2" (1 cm), 5/8" (1.5 cm), or 3/4" (2 cm) Ribbon (to fit size of box)
- 27" (68.5 cm) of mini garland
- Assorted mini holiday flowers, berries, or greenery

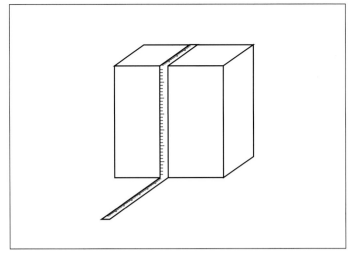

1 Measure all around the length (long side) of the box and add 1" (2.5 cm). Write this measurement on the paper.

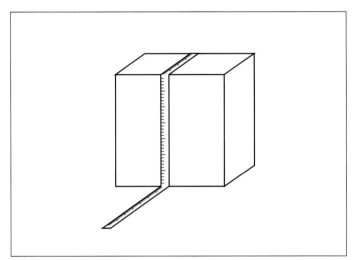

2 Now measure all around the width (short side) of the box and add 1" (2.5 cm). Write this measurement on the paper.

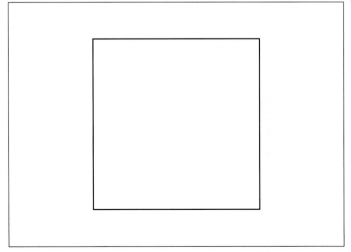

3 Use these measurements to cut out the Washi.

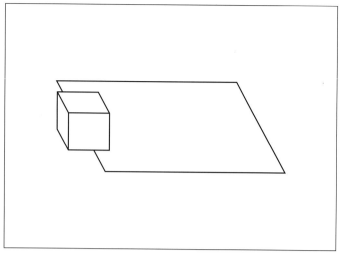

4 Place the printed Washi wrong side up on the table. Position the gift box off the edge of the printed Washi, at one of the narrow ends.

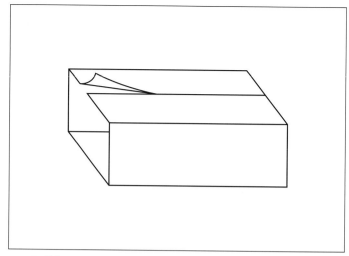

5 Roll box over Washi to cover it until the paper overlaps at the other end.

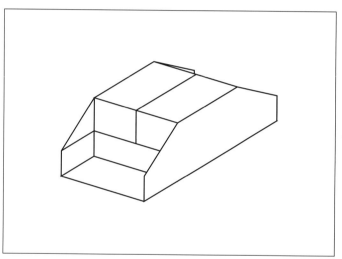

6 Fold in the sides, following the illustration, adding tape to keep it in place.

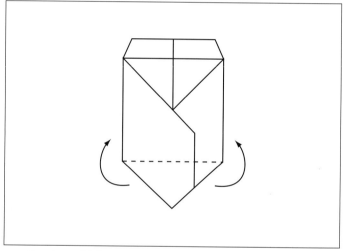

7 Continue folding in the sides until as illustrated.

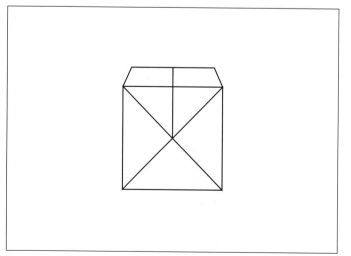

8 Both ends should meet nicely in the center, as illustrated. Add tape as needed to keep the Washi in place.

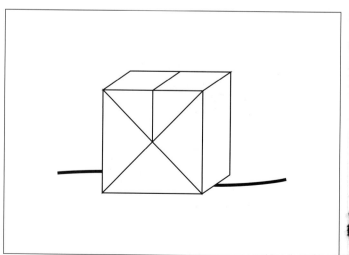

9 Place ribbon on the table and position the gift box, wrong side up, in the center.

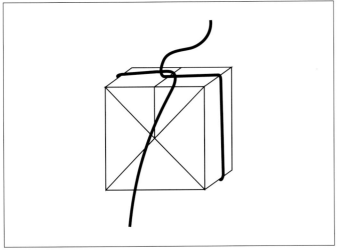

10 Cross the ribbon over itself and bring toward the opposite side. See illustration for guidance.

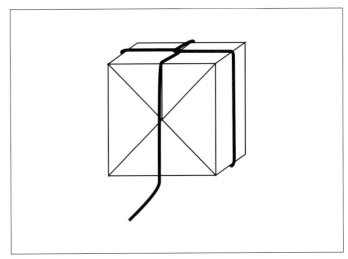

11 Flip gift box over.

12 Tie a bow, gathering up three coils of mini garland with the remaining ribbon.

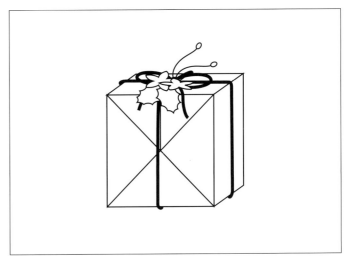

13 Hot glue or tie in other holiday greenery or flowers around and under the garland.

14 Add a coordinating gift label (see page 92).

Easy Gift Labels

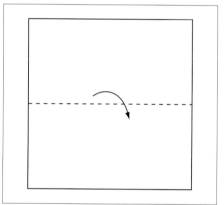

1 Trace the printed Washi paper pattern of your choice.

2 Fold the two 6" x 3" (15 x 7.5 cm) rectangles of printed Washi in half. Open them back up and apply glue stick to one side, then fold the halves back together and press to secure.

Add a personal touch of class to any gift with these creative labels. They can also be used to tie a gift bag, enriching plain brown lunch bags or ordinary plastic bags. Easy to make, these labels are a wonderful way to make use of your Washi scraps.

EQUIPMENT AND MATERIALS FOR ONE GIFT LABEL

- Two 6" x 3" (15 x 7.5 cm) rectangles of printed Washi
- 6" x 3" (15 x 7.5 cm) rectangle of regular white or cream paper
- Covered florist stem wire (12" / 30.5 cm) cut into two 6" (15 cm) pieces
- Tracing paper and pencil
- Small sharp scissors
- Ruler or measuring tape
- Glue stick
- Paper clips
- Metallic pens

3 Paper clip the traced Washi pattern to the glued pieces of printed Washi and cut out. You should have two patterns cut out.

ASSORTED GIFT LABEL PATTERNS

Copy the pattern using tracing paper and a pencil.

Poinsettia Printed Washi Pattern

Poinsettia Paper Pattern

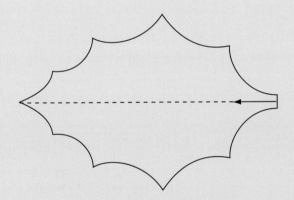

Holly Leaf Printed Washi Pattern

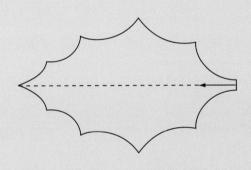

Holly Leaf Paper Pattern

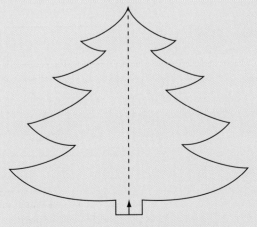

Christmas Tree Printed Washi Pattern

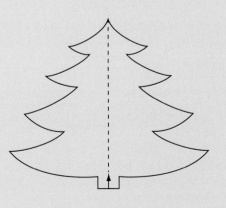

Christmas Tree Paper Pattern

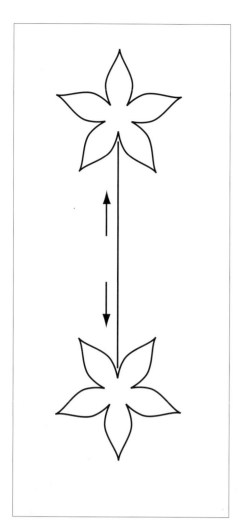

4 Carefully open up the indicated Washi ends on the pattern. Insert the florist wire into the opening and push the wire down the middle, nearly to the other end. Close back up and press together and let it dry while you cut out the white paper patterns.

5 Trace the corresponding white paper pattern.

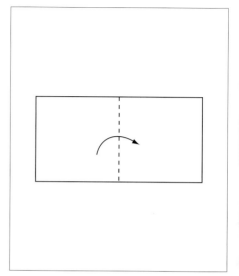

6 Fold the piece of paper in half, paper clip it to the pattern, and cut out. You should have two patterns cut out.

7 Paste each white paper pattern to one side of each wired printed Washi tie to make a label. Use the metallic pen to write your holiday message. Add bows or other small decorative items.

Acknowledgments

As I study Washi paper's quiet and unobtrusive progression through centuries of Japanese experience, I stand in awe of the impact it has made, not only on Japan but now on the entire world. During that progression it played a key role throughout the development of the country, touching every feature of Japanese life. I have learned that over the years, a close relationship between papermaker and paper users developed, resulting in Washi becoming an integral part of the Japanese culture. As a result of this progression the skills that have been passed down from generation to generation produced a functional, yet extraordinary paper that reflected the soul and spirit of Japan. Japan today has mastered the art of living with the best of both worlds by infusing centuries of tradition into the modern technological world we live in today.

The traditional aspects of Washi crafting are being adapted—or adopted—in people's daily lives as creative Washi projects are being displayed at international exhibitions, art fairs, and workshops throughout America and the Western world. The reputation of this handmade Japanese paper is growing by leaps and bounds because of its versatility, beauty, and power as an expressive medium that appeals to the visual, tactile, and emotional senses of crafters all over the world.

My Washi craft journey has taken a relatively small amount of time in comparison and continues to be dependent upon the involvement of my students and colleagues—those wonderful individuals, young and old, who sit in my Washi classes and dare to venture into the abstract world of Washi to create new and exciting works of art. Without their patience and eagerness it would have been utterly impossible to

continue the Washi journey. Their support and continued encouragement has enabled us to navigate into new territory in Washi creativity and style. To all of them I owe a great deal of gratitude and appreciation. They truly are global partners in the world of Washi crafts. Through Washi crafts, the bridge of friendship and understanding between many cultures continues to be the high point of all classes, gatherings, and social settings.

I want to also acknowledge Tuttle Publishing for its support and insightful promotion of the beautiful Washi craft. I thank my editor Amanda Dupuis for her expertise, enthusiasm, and hard work in bringing *Holiday Paper Crafts from Japan* to print.

Finally, I dedicate this book to my families, the Uhls and the Boarmans.

—Robertta A. Uhl
Okinawa, Japan